Discipline

Park

Discipline Park

Toby Altman

Wendy's Subway

CONTENTS

MANDATORY FIELDS (a memoir)

"Wherefrom fall

all architectures I am”

—Robert Duncan

fig. 1. I want to write an essay on scarcity. To describe the city as an effect of deletion or decay: a shadow, a graveyard, a series of imaginary islands. I would begin, for instance, with the graves in Lincoln Park. I would say how the park was stripped of its corpses to make it clean and safe, a place where money stays. Or I would write about Daniel Burnham, who asked the city to build a harp of garbage in the lake. Who has time for that? I too live on trash. A woman's face with an orange price tag on it. $7.99. A book of coupons. Wild onion collapsing in the throat. And what if the meek refuse to inherit?

healing grasses

to draw an object: "Centuries ago it was customary to celebrate the beginning of a building with a corner stone when men suspected construction had gone far enough to be noticed by the Gods. In this day of ecological concerns, we continue this same ceremony with a topping stone to announce to heaven that we will encroach no further on their space. We have gone as high as we intend to."
—Bertrand Goldberg

I want to write about the city as extension, delay, a limb that buds from the body of the police. To argue that architecture transforms sound into substance. I would say, "We are all sheltered in suffering noise." I want to ask, as elegantly as possible: "In what does human life consist?" And I would give a savage answer: it is a traveling wound, which inflicts itself on the landscape. As a child I was taught to draw an object by fleshing the dark around it. In this way, I learned to think of the body as a luminous institution, an unmarked space where money travels. I want to ask, "Is a world without scarcity still a world?" And then refuse to answer.

---

cannot help

fig. 2. I ate alone at Potbelly and I was not nourished. I watched the institution demolish the hospital where I was born, unfolding as it goes into the raw open, unfathomed wound, and I was not nourished. I watched it again, and I was not nourished. At the time, I drew a small monthly stipend from the institution, and yet I was not nourished. I fell on the ice and my shoulder caught me. The fall lingered in my shoulder, a stuckness that would not nourish. In fact, the wound advanced through the house until it became hard abundance of leaf. Still, I was not nourished.

I was born in Prentice Women's Hospital: Designed by Bertrand Goldberg between 1969 and 1975, the building was a landmark of architectural Brutalism. After a protracted fight, it was demolished by Northwestern University in 2014 to make space for a glassy new research tower. "I know that Bertrand Goldberg's vision is alive in Chicago beyond one building," wrote Mayor Rahm Emanuel, defending his support for the demolition of the building. "We must promote . . . the future." I worked for Northwestern at the time and I continue to work there. I tell anyone who asks that this is a "cruel allegory of neoliberalism." Is there any other kind of allegory left?

---

it's kind of my thing

On the phone, my father asked: "How does your labor read as sorrow?" My labor does not nourish, I said. The poem acts as the institution's hammer. It tears without repair. It ends by making the body fruitful. "What does a body nourish?" he asked. "Obviously time heals no wounds. Obviously it multiplies the mouth. It can be cured only by the end of life." Why do I seek the living? Because they do not nourish. All winter I stopped my eyes and ears with dense paper. All winter I promised myself: this mouth is dread. Nothing no longer can be said. Still, I was not nourished.

fig. 3. "Concrete starts life as a messy soup of suspended dust, grits and slumpy aggregate." It ends as rubble: the point of wreckage that enjambs the river. It rots from the inside. Its weakness is its reinforcement. The stiff rebar that helps it stand. Its authors thought it would never decay. They thought they had designed permanence itself. Beyond which there is only winter. A U-Haul roosting at the far end of the hospital. It is frail skin sculpted to hold. It is a pocket where property goes. Who knows what happens inside it, probably language in its liquid form.

brutal

I attempt a bureaucratic aesthetic: writing that resonates within measured frequencies of feeling. Which serves to administer pleasure in manageable doses. Which displays its structural material. Writing that reinforces the concrete where it sags and splinters. I mean: it takes on the qualities and status of an apparition. Incompleteness. Anonymity. Horizontality. "All writing should lacerate the limbs that bind it to language," I wrote in my notebook. I don't remember why.

"The point is to see the body," Simone says. Can you see my body yet. How about now. I want my body to happen to me, the way concrete is poured in a wooden frame and hardens there, taking the texture of the wood simply because that's how it makes itself, how it happens to act. All forms of deliberate motion can be very beautiful. Simone taught me that. One body is a sculpture. Two bodies are a landscape. Three bodies are a building. After that you're on your own.

---

vernacular

fig. 4. **At the institution a woman tells me, "I don't know where my body is going." I too descend into muteness. I too disappear into the lens. "The step of the wandering Jew is in every son," Djuna says. My language is a state of exile. While my students look away, I massage the stony edge of my shoulder. This kind of touching makes the knot sharper. "This kind of stone cannot learn," the institution says, "to be tender." With my stipend, I buy hot pads and ice packs. I strip my shirt and lay them on my shoulder. Now the knot is loose. In the world as such.**

strangled

Bertrand was a Jew and so am I, sort of. When I was sixteen, my family traveled to our shtetl, Stolbtsy, in Belarus. We saw teenagers drag racing around a statue of Stalin. We saw the river where my great-grandfather, Abraham, and his father shipped timber. A patriarch with a patriarch's name. My aunt bent down to take a vial of the water with her. This town, that he fled. To escape conscription in the Russian Army. To write about it is like pouring water back and forth between empty jars. In the final stages of his dementia, Abraham slipped loose from English and spoke flawlessly the Russian of his youth. Both languages being the language of exile. To write with it is like pouring water back and forth between empty jars.

Don't tell me that isn't lovely.
Don't tell me that isn't loss.
One self is a winter.
All my other self is gone.
"Wherever you meet him,"
(Djuna again), "you feel
that he has come from . . .
some country that he has
devoured
rather than resided in."

----

lamp

Eileen says language has two functions:
inventory and prophecy. Like money,
all it says is loss.
In this film, the institution's money
is visible as a series of cuttings.
It slowly severs the tendon
from the ankle. It pierces without
reprieve or repair. "That's nice,"
says the institution. "Now replace 'it' with 'I.'"

fig. 5. Now my shoulder is hunted throughout. It becomes a hill of frost. I refuse to unfold its interior sweetness. The soft centrality that language nourishes. I refuse to unfold. Instead, I write the word *wound*. Then I write it again. Is this a way of making it behave? Do I want to multiply its penetration? Well, do I. Every entrance is a weapon. Every entrance is a wound. I write the wound I lack. I lack the dark audacity to let myself be fucked. To open as a city opens. To anyone who wants to come.

it's how you're

This kind of geography is contagious.
This kind of landscape has been
carefully organized as a packaged
thinness. An intrinsic tendency
toward orderly repetition. To reduce
everything to simple, abstract, material
volumes. To expose, accentuate,
and toughen the elements of simple
building. Creases and pleats,
spars of brute concrete.
In this way, architecture becomes
a journey without arrival.
The communal task of total war. Does it end?
It ends by making the camera feeling.

---

evidence

“[B]rutalism doesn’t so much recede into
as realign its environment.
It is about preparing
the paths and platforms
that enable and ennoble
even the most mundane
of human actions.”
—Keith Krumweide

fig. 6. This is a score for a dance. You hold a ball of paper between your head and the head of another dancer. The paper is dry and loose. It is heavy and wet. It exceeds itself, it is itself again. You may not touch it with your hands. Only your shoulders. Only your head. Only your neck. You may touch your partner. You may treat them as a living bottle. A container of raw interior. Together, you cross a large space, carrying the paper between you. Then you come back. You may stop at any time. You may ask yourself a series of questions: i.e., When does the absence of motion become the presence of dance? How can I make my head into a hand? At a certain point, the paper becomes an organ of perception, a gift from one dancer to another. It says who is wounded and where. In this way, it is a sense

"The Brutalist citizen,
therefore, has to be understood as an
abstract, egalitarian ideal

of place. It says, "Some of the city is grief and some of it is not." The dancer takes this grief upon herself. She becomes an antenna that registers the traffic of heroin and handguns, petcoke, hog meat, and human bodies. This frail antenna. This wound in the thigh of the world. And all the eyes of the audience made loose by desire. You become an antenna and the antenna collapses. You look at Facebook and think about nothing. You walk into a building and the building injures you because architecture is an affliction of the fluids, is the sharp fluid that washes the face away. Your situation is facelessness. What you need is a way of making the face happen to itself. You are dancing against a screen of concrete, architecture of grief. This is what makes the dance last. Eventually your body will ask: can we not.

---

without a face

not as an individual
lost in the concrete
cave of some
gargantuan building."
—Jack Self

fig. 7. **The bruise of the fall put**
my shoulder out of joint.
This kind of falling is contagious.
The grinding passes into the earth.
For a week, or maybe more,
spars of raw concrete
pierce the mirror. Afterward,
I began to conceive of the ground
as a weapon. I wrote in my notebook,
"The stone is / absorbed / in / the staircase."
It does not permit mutation or break.
Its pain is legible. As a collar.

His career begins as a series of experiments: with the affordances of the material. Cheap, ubiquitous materials. He designed, for instance, a railcar made of plywood instead of steel and a mobile ice cream parlor that unfolds from a central mast. The material remains, even in his mature work, cheap and ubiquitious: concrete, which is made from whatever happens to be at hand, like rubble, gravel, sand. Taking the texture of the place where it was cast.

---

suddenly piercing

I thought the future would bring a place of succulence and denial. Cold cuts and lemonade. A perishing retail center. Instead, it promises gradual release. Into a brightly lit institutional space. In which the armored personnel carrier appears. As an elegant vessel for the divine. The dense spirit who speaks, when he speaks at all, in emulsified cement. This is what he says. I stand in the bottomless event and translate the staircase back into stone. There is nothing to see here.

fig. 8. I learned to seek liberty in restraint. At the time of this writing, all forms of liberation were suspect anyway. The landscape began to be confused with the bodies interred within it. So that, in my notebook, I described a mass grave as a "pubic marsh" and apparently meant it. Of course, an unclaimed body belongs to the state. And when it is touched by the state, it turns into the state's witness. "Somehow no one is guilty," it announces to the court. Then, just for good measure: "I am not guilty. I own a late model Prius and my debts are mostly taken care of." Same.

exuberant

I wrote a book about marriage called *idk but it works for me*. I showed my friends photos of slaughtered buildings and said: "Imagine Hillary Clinton with the TNT pump or pushing the red button." The question, I said, is not how to salvage the past, but how to destroy it ethically. My friends began to ask, with real concern, if I "liked" Brutalism. I was embarrassed. As though confessing a fetish. I like its honesty, I told them. At least it does not lie to you. At least it tells you what an institution is. An institution is a reasonable amount of cash and a safe place to hide it. Every other architecture I know tries to conceal this fact or make it beautiful.

---

bureaucracy

"It is a strange paradox that the benign ideology of the welfare state chose to be represented by an architectural style known as Brutalism. The market economy takes the exact opposite approach, concealing an essentially brutal rule behind a seemingly benign, 'politically correct' architectural language—survival of the fittest under the guise of common taste."

—Reinier de Graaf and Laura Baird

fig. 9. Thus, I adopt a lawyered tone: tough, unnutritious, resistant to prettiness. All my work a kind of nausea, or a kind of longing. Longing for a language that can't be said. A language that does not damage. Built like the socket of a shoulder, flexible and sturdy, fresh ligament. So that its uses are holding and turning, raising and lifting, caress. In fact, it is a question of building: how to make a flowering place. Landscape of seduction and restraint. That contains "a silent space / for the rhythmic movement of heart and / lungs." Think of it as a nursery, an asylum, a hospital: a refuge for someone who does

utopia

In *Capitalist Realism*, Mark Fisher notes a "widespread sense that not only is capitalism the only viable political and economic system, but that it is now impossible even to imagine a coherent alternative to it." Let's say you agree. Doesn't that mean that utopia is the task of poetry, that the poet is called to freshness and conjecture, adventurous song that soars beyond the limits of the world? What do you see up there—I am asking you, almost in prayer—and what kind of language do you need to tell me about it?

not yet exist. Now, when I am shaving or applying deodorant, I try to imagine its patients. How limitless their bodies might be: unbottled jelly, dense with amino acids and anti-depressants. They take, exactly, the shape of feeling. They repel every kind of wounding. Imperceptible and fragrant, they attach themselves to the bitter part of language and suck it out, all the rest remaining hot. Then again, maybe not. This kind of body doesn't cost a lot. Its price is no. Its price is not.

----

of no

fig. 10. The institution asks you to teach a class called "How to Be Lonely." Funny you should ask. You stand in front of your students, dressed in your best pants, and offer them eight lessons in loneliness. In the first lesson, you confess you feel no desire to renew life. You prize the dead—the minute action of their pens. By the second lesson, you have no students left. Should you continue? The institution does not answer your repeated emails. You present your second lesson to an empty room. In the second lesson, you describe the statue of Ceres atop the Board of Trade Building. She hangs above your city, swoon of silver, and she sings. Translated into the language of the living, her song is sweetness of commerce

displacement

In one of Bertrand's early drawings, Prentice rises off thick columns: blunt teeth or vestigial lungs. Then it learns not to breathe. In another, it stands on a series of delicate legs, tucked beneath the tower's mass. The sky appears as thick marrow. The heart is a bitter angle. Each drawing is somehow incompatible with the world—unbuildable, or at least unbuilt. I look at these drawings alone in an archive. The archive is illegible. It provides a language of structure and support: *Typical / Except / Plastic Glazing*. Each drawing acts as a score for my unfolding. I begin to feel unfolded. Unfolded, I live "calf-deep / in debris." "Well, I don't have any more nachos in my belly," someone's dad announces in the archive's bathroom as he washes his hands. Then his buddy laughs.

---

park

or information. Suffused with libido. As if she wished to caress the stocks exchanged beneath her. You try to reproduce her song for the class. "All my life / longing / to be / a wife," you sing. Your voice is like bruised glass. After the second lesson, the institution politely asks you to refrain. You refuse to refrain. For the third lesson, you take your class on a field trip to a slaughterhouse. "How does it feel to be in the presence of this building?" you ask an empty school bus. Frankly, ok. You read from the guide book, "The building got its form entirely / from the functional / requirements of movement / of cattle / and the evisceration process." As though compelled by the frenzy of the slaughter, you begin to dance. Your arms and legs resemble a prison in their intricate locking and unlocking. Now you are always dancing.

fig. 11. **Idea for a performance: four cylinders of concrete are poured on a podium. This may be accomplished by an invisible hand. It may be the effect of an inaccessible past. Or, the performance may deploy the bodies of men in overalls and hard hats, nakedly apparent to the audience. They create an interior, a space for flowering. They undress the city around them. They display, as if for the first time, the way the city frames and subdues the swamp. How each building on the grid cuts a space where the air, wounded by compaction, bitterly flourishes.**

my career

---

four cylinders of concrete are poured on a podium: At Prentice, a single core supported the whole weight of the building. The exterior vaulted off the interior. Similarly, each room on each floor was designed to be visible from a central nursing station, but screened from its surroundings. It takes, as its spatial model, a wheel of birth control. It is "a mill for grinding rouges honest." Panopticon of tenderness. In this way, the limb is sustained by the abundance of the body. In this way, the building is a cure machine.

----

is grief

Idea for a performance: this was the architecture of everyone. Thankfully, it belongs to the institution. The institution announces to the press, "FOREVER is LOSS whatever." Idea for a performance: I take its money anyway. It becomes the wound I live with, cancer tourist. Idea for a performance: sometimes during sex, I rehearse my failures, setbacks, and regrets. This produces the desired effect: i.e., every day I am more abundant and so is my rent. Meanwhile my body gentrifies the bed. Everything it touches turns posthumous white. Idea for a performance: everyone is exhausted and no one has time.

fig. 12. Imagine a building that inflicts persistent, escalating pain. Like language, this pain cannot be located in a single organ; it is mobile and infectious. Within this building, cancer blossoms in the lung. The kidney chokes. Promiscuous growth inside a butcher's knife. All in the time it takes to make a pot of coffee or go to the bathroom. Now imagine a city composed entirely of such buildings, differently scaled for various uses. Each building, a site of religious ecstasy, a bathhouse, or a nursery. Each building, radiating asphalt and ozone. Pain in aerosol doses.

proposal

"Architecture, in anyone's definition of it, exists primarily to be at the service of the body" (Gins and Arakawa). The architect measures a series of mundane acts: frying a cut of steak, going to the bathroom in the middle of the night, making love (lying down or standing up). He uses that phrase exactly, "making love," to keep the building in the frame of matrimony. Where love is implied, as a furnace implies a network of pipes and ducts: intrinsic to the building, diffusing pleasure and warmth everywhere. In this way, a building is ready for a person whether a person is there or not.

First this city is a seed of glass, stationed in the liver. Then the ash can and the arc lamp gather. They deposit colonies of nerve throughout, which infest the bedspread and the bed. In short: the whole has the softness of numbers. In short: the whole is draped in an electric net, unskinned nerve span. The citizens of this city return the pain they receive in equivalent doses. Each of their acts, however mundane, inflicts shipwreck on the city. In this city, pain is tender economy. In this city, pain is passage. Transit without reprieve. Pain is a loss of pattern. No. Pain is pattern without loss.

fig. 13. **Imagine another city, in which pain has been rigorously segregated from the population. This city is architecture without loneliness, architecture without need. Its walls and windows double as lymphatic ditches, so that injury and affliction drain into a landfill or a supermarket, just beyond the city's boundaries. Soft mountain which breeds with bacterial logic. Each year, some citizens dredge and expand its precincts: a practice of surrender that makes the world at large. The rest are wrapped in structural plastic. Each of them requires ubiquitous surveillance. Even a scratch might bleed indefinitely. In this way, the city is designed to amplify contagion, flameless cremation.**

proposal

"Sometimes dream is so rampant, so wild
As to seem more luxuriant than day's repose
So without riot spreading everywhere
How can I be both here and there?"
—Bernadette Mayer

for a radiant city

Now imagine a body that belongs to both of these cities at once. Everything it touches becomes architecture. A stripe of mortar swells inside its throat. It checks its phone compulsively. It goes to the institution to teach a series of introductory courses. It scrapes the uterine wall for signs of washing. It wrings out a washcloth in the sink. It seeks surrogate release, gray water radiating in the drain. It is anywhere armored, fullness without edges. Breathlessness instead of breathlessly. If I email my students in the middle of the night to tell them I am in pain, how will they know which city has captured me? I am different things in different places. I am between distances. "So without riot spreading everywhere / How can I be both here and there?"

fig. 14. I receive an email from the institution, asking for its money. "Dear Toby," it says, "Your voice is still missing." At the institution, I ask intimate questions like, "Who is speaking here?" "Do objects suffer?" "How can a wound be compassionately designed?" This is a condition of my money. I use these questions to own blocks of cheddar and bags of cereal. Shards of meat and shattered grain. Impossible to eat without making the carcass fruitful. Each eating puts a little nowhere in me. Each eating makes me. Palpable debt material. I buy these things and then my mouth becomes their cage. Come in and see the future of banking.

carnivorous

At the institution, a white man tells me, "There is no freedom to enjoy." If you say so. He uses the language of flourishing. "Are you trying to be in the room with many kinds of loss and presence?" he asks. I want to ask, "What kind of sex is left, and do I like it?" I want to say, "I am useful and straight. Last night I urged my wife to sew the word 'perishable' onto a pillow case." She thinks this poem does not adequately announce its complicity. In the violence I am trying to name. "This is an essay on repetition," the white man says. Then: "There is no such thing."

---

wage

A white man tells me: This particular white man is Lee Edelman, during a 2015 lecture at Northwestern called "There Is No Freedom to Enjoy" (on Harriet Jacobs's *Incidents in the Life of a Slave Girl*). His argument, best I can recall, was that the demands of freedom and the demands of pleasure are irreconcilable. We can have one but not the other. Hence, we all live, as Jacobs writes about antebellum America, in a "house of unclean birds." Nothing really heals. A night of sharp sleep puts the twist back in my shoulder. My grandfather, the surgeon, liked to say, "All bleeding stops." This was a joke. A surgical joke. All bleeding stops. Maybe not.

“Being different

—Sun Chips

BRUISE SMUT

is our thing."

"We asked the consultants to take a thorough look at what might be possible in terms of reusing the building as research space, but it just won't work," Nayler said. "The building has a number of problems and its configuration doesn't lend itself well to adaptive reuse. As a result, it would be an extremely inefficient building in terms of usable space, even if it could be effectively renovated."
—"STUDY: OLD PRENTICE HOSPITAL NOT POSSIBLE FOR REUSE,"
Northwestern News, May 25, 2011.

fig. 1. **Only the dead feast on images. Only the image is a balm in lead: always budding, so that each season ends with the leading brand of beauteous roof. Now my friends are roses of shadow, roses of shade, lapped in lead. As a child, I stole a stone-hard pear and let it rot under my bed. As a child, I came to identify with the camera, the way it frames the human body. As a garden of melting petroleum.**

nature no longer

has any use for us

Upon closer inspection, with instruments more powerful than the genital eye, it disaggregates into a fulsome garden. Fields of thistle and wet asparagus. Bonsey bitter and cordial lavender. Meanwhile, the plastic is burned into its flesh—forming, as it were, a suture. It signifies a tongue. An exposition of dark speech. All its receipts were found, under trial, to be falsified.

“Chicago can find tomorrow’s cures, if we let it.”
—“Finding Tomorrow’s Cures,” *Northwestern University*, n.d.

fig. 2. **Departure closed us in an immense silence. We were occasionally obliged to touch. Kissing and caressing. Married to the lock. “Never believe that a smooth space will save us,” you said. No, you didn’t. “She holds the architecture that holds her,” you said. “Its material is proximity to blue.” You were unable to supply the name. You became a voice in another room. Rooting in shit, branches of white fruit.**

clap your hands if you feel

The film begins to crumble, even if it's played backward. Which means: morning is here or soon to arrive. Its material is proximity to sleep. "Closed in an immense silence," you said. "We prepare to die in agony," you said. No. We have decided not to die.

like a room without a roof

"Goldberg believed that progressive architectural ideas would be accepted in a consumer democracy only if they were more affordable than traditional solutions—affordability made radical design possible….[He] understood the need for new social and architectural ideals to be integrated within rather than placed in opposition to capitalism."
—Igor Marjanović and Katerina Rüedi Ray

fig. 3. Like a lucid window,
this image presents an eye
whose gaze is also the origin
of light. The eye observes
itself in the act of threshing.
The act requires a lubricant:
vegetative oil that travels
through the open window
and folds the space
in its warm lengthening.

Before it means anything else,
an idea is a kind of seeing.
It sometimes behaves
like a lamp in a closed room.
An eye amplifies itself
in language. It carries
with it the juicy kingdom
of the tendon and the jaw.

groin

----

vault

**“There” is a unit of time.
It has been reinforced by steel rods.
This is called the concrete.
It is occupied by business travelers
with dollarous faces. At the bank,
I heard an advertisement
for a bank. “Hello, kitchen
of my dreams,” said a luscious voice.
A voice trained to lubricate money.
Hello, cancerous underwear.
A window is a wise veil.**

“Construction of new medical research facilities on the site of old Prentice will help us reach our goal of becoming a top ten medical center, and will help provide state-of-the-art health care in the Chicago area,” Sunshine said. “In addition, it is estimated that a new facility would bring in more than $200 million in additional research funding and provide over 2,000 full time jobs.”
—“NOT POSSIBLE”

"This document lays out clearly both the University's plans and the growing support for them," said Eugene S. Sunshine, senior vice president for business and finance. "Our goals are to conduct lifesaving research in a state-of-the-art new facility and, in doing so, create jobs, fuel the Chicago economy and ensure the health of Chicago-area residents."
—Alan Cubbage, "Case for New Biomedical Research Center on Site of Former Prentice Hospital," *Northwestern News*, October 3, 2012.

fig. 4. **Unfortunately, friends, the future is on fire. Melodious presence of a flame. Thus a building is a wild jar. A building is about to happen. The word itself describes a flexing, pull of steel into shape. Ongoing, unstable, in pain. In other words, it ends in desolation. The lovely spine turns tender. There is no meat that gathers on it. There is no human salvage. No medicinal touch. The building makes its final**

arrangements in the dust. Even the thought of it makes flesh religiously. Makes limitless emergency. When a verdict comes (a verdict always does), it robs us of our witness. "You've been leaving yourself everywhere," says the judge. Then, "You are free to have nothing." Then, "Freedom is sad." In other words, the future is warm with loss. Is there too much of it or just enough?

---

mortgage

it robs us of our witness: In an article on the sculpture of Doris Salcedo, Cathy Park Hong writes, "When the verdict was announced, one felt robbed of one's eyes." She is writing about the non-indictment of Darren Wilson, the white policeman who murdered Michael Brown. What better demonstration of the cruel magic of racism, the way that it subtracts the agent from the act?

Etymologically, a "hospital" is a house for pilgrims, travelers, and strangers—an asylum for the destitute. "A house for corporate lodging," the OED suggests. The word does not imply wounding until relatively late, around the thirteenth century. Then, as if contagious, the wound spreads through all its senses.

fig. 5. **Alone in the creamy wilderness**
of the hotel, I become water in agony:
a mobile home with its walls unwelded.
As if to stabilize myself,
to dress the puncture in medicinal plastic,
I focus on the shard, filmed with delectation.
I taste the perishing feast.

"The new research center will help us continue to attract more of the world's best research minds and clinicians and help secure additional research grants. It would also put our city on the map as a leader in the field of medical research, a distinction that would benefit the community as well as the University and its hospital affiliates," said Eric Neilson, MD, dean of Northwestern's Feinberg School of Medicine and vice president for medical affairs. —"Support Sought for Expansion Plan on Old Prentice Site," *Northwestern News*, August 29, 2012.

terminal

- -

---

beach

Outside, wild muck burdens every bow.
A swan is hunting the banks
of the drainage ditch.
Grime reaper, she rides a loaf
of fertilizer foam. There is a blank
between her fleshing eyes. The kind
that likes to be fructified. As it happens,
I was thinking like a corporation that winter.
I bent the slow, objective lens to stimulate
my appetite for debt. Thus, the hiatus
in my flesh expanded according
to a cancerous logic. My hands asked
for the suturing harp. They returned
to my lap, empty.

"Northwestern's plans call for construction of 300,000 to 500,000 square feet of research space starting in 2015 with eventual build-out of approximately 1.2 million square feet. A group of preservationists has objected to the University's plans, calling for the former hospital to be landmarked. However, the site of the now-vacant former Prentice Women's Hospital is at the heart of the University's plans, Northwestern officials said."

—Cubbage, "Case for New"

fig. 6. I was caressed by the tongue of the clock. I lay upon the embalming table. I became skilled in the use of surgical mirrors. As if to dismantle a painting by washing it, very carefully, in oil. When I mixed my labor with the land, it became pregnant with polymers and paint. At the far verge of opacity, I stripped the pasture to show the process of luminous building. I made a cut and my fingers followed through it.

attractive

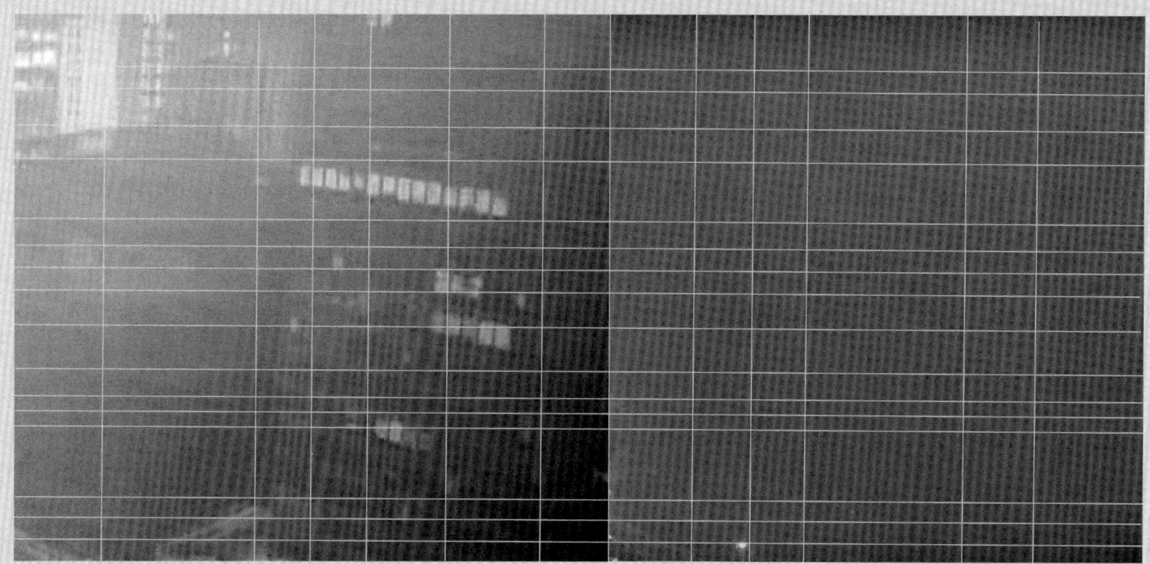

What is this "bloody-minded architecture" that pierces the solid core protecting the genitals? That penetrates with ineloquence to sculpt a formal clarity in the break? This building is made of what it appears to be made of. Rather than whitewash, the lucid glaze of animal fat, etc. It gathers all gazing to itself. Now it is an outbreak. In the vanilla.

---

to capital

***bloody-minded architecture*: Rayner Banham from his 1955 essay, "The New Brutalism": "In the last resort what characterizes the New Brutalism in architecture as in painting is precisely its brutality, its *je-m'en-foutisme*, its bloody-mindedness. . . Here is a building," he continues, discussing Louis Kahn's Yale Art Center, "which is uncompromisingly frank about its materials, which is inconceivable apart from its boldly exhibited structural method . . ."**

"Architects disagree
on whether or not to give
old Prentice landmark status.
Architects do not agree
on the worthiness
of giving landmark status
to old Prentice.
In fact, most architects
would agree
that Marina City
is a better example
of Bertrand Goldberg's work."
—"Finding Tomorrow's Cures"

real

---

fig. 7. **I have an iPhone
and the battery is not
what it used to be.
I buy smooth-wrought
hummus for dipping
and snacking. I eat
a pizza called
"Smack Your Spinach."
I am sitting at the tyrant's table.
And the tyrant says,
"You won't find an ATM
trekking through a canyon
but you will almost
anywhere else."
Ok, but can I use your bathroom.
Under the pressure of the camera
he becomes a white
knife: an agony, a propensity
to be injured.
Even as he urges the wound.**

Is this creature in agony?
How should I know?
The tool suffers
the same fate as the master.
Each season ends
with a spectacular corpse:
the tyrant, whose body
cannot be counted.
An untimely fig,
shaken from the branch.
The tyrant says,
"Politics is an organized sense of dread."
No, exercise after thirty
is an organized sense of dread.
No, the self is dread
by other means. Usually
the world is a weapon.
Isn't the weapon wonderful.

The tool suffers the same fate as the master: I believe this is quoted from Marx, but I forget where. In the absence of precise citation, treat it as a prayer. An invocation of ruin. At a poetics conference, I write in my notes, "This poem's [sic] thesis is 'Fuck Rahm Emanuel.'" Not sure which poem. Not many poems. The speaker says over and over, "My time is running out." "My time is running out." My time is running out.

---

talk

fig. 8. **In pornography, an image implies a sequel, a chain of revelations. The eye is slowly unclothed. It shows the absence of what was there. It shows you how to look. When I look, the world is wounded water. Quietly running out. Everywhere stripped of its greenness, stripped of its sovereignty. Vents on the crown of the landfill. Am I doing it right? Just text me when you're close.**

i want to say what is lost

---

i want to say what is lost

---

i want to say what is lost

---

i want to say what is lost

"Statement on Prentice Lawsuit Dismissal," ***Northwestern News*****,** **February 7, 2013**

i want to say what is lost

"Northwestern University is pleased that the Chicago Commission on Landmarks today voted to reject giving final landmark status to the former Prentice Women's Hospital building, which is now owned by the University. We appreciate very much the thoughtful consideration that the commissioners and staff of the Chicago Commission on Landmarks, Mayor Rahm Emanuel and Alderman Brendan Reily have given to this issue."

---

what is lost

---

what is lost

---

what is lost

---

what is lost

Um, according to Google, I'm in a green emptiness, a place without borders or roads. I break at both ends and no one knows the boundary. I'm cleaning the crown of the flowers to keep the flies off. I'm setting out the iris even though its owner is away. I could not give an answer I was so strangled by grief. I'm always seeing. Through the eye of another.

"Northwestern University is pleased to learn that two preservation groups have moved for a voluntary dismissal of their lawsuit regarding the decision by the City of Chicago not to give landmark status to the former Prentice Women's Hospital."
— "Statement on Dismissal"

fig. 9. **What is the future for Oedipus, whose eyes stream blue petroleum juice? Yes, let us speak of the future. Even after such a massacre of concrete. It involves, simply, being in pain. Its consequence is the progressive destruction of wetlands and meadows. Its promise is the orderly placement of roses and ivy. A dead rabbit tossed on a bed of barley. It engages the manufacture of bags and bottles, mourning silks, disposable nylons,**

blister

the progressive destruction of wetlands and meadows: Bertrand worked at a time when it seemed likely (even necessary) that Chicago would dissolve into grassy islands, cellular suburbs, linked by long miles of tarmac. A pasture without a center. Unlike the architects of my generation, Goldberg was not a global figure, hopping from city to city, building magnificent, isolated skyscrapers. His work is here, most of it anyway. He invests in the city: finite, dense, enthusiastically hurt.

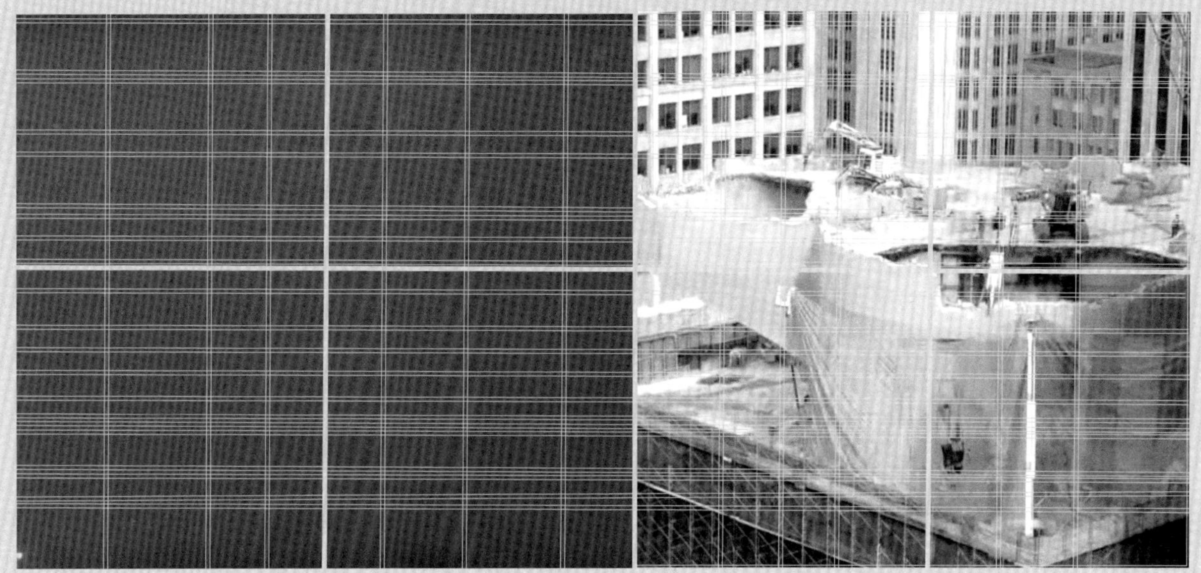

pack

the tissue that spools out inside of children as they learn the rudiments of language. The future, for them, is a bottomless event: a very deep pizza pie, folded into or inscribed within their inky, pathological matter. "Behold," they say, "I lay upon the stony bridal bed and all my sensuous characteristics were extinguished." All day, they refrained from creating value. And gunfire was their food. "Behold," they say, "I have become a weapon."

fig. 10. **In this image,**
the tender structure
begins to melt.
The medium itself
is disposable,
delicately glassed
substance, through
which the camera
issues its intricate
forms of unevenness.

Consider the dark round
of the open lens.
The person who holds
it is organized, violently,
into a glassy stream.
And only the banker's
eye survives,
like a low drum
in the meadow.
Whose meaning is:

refrain.

hospital

The history of which I speak
is merely “wreckage on wreckage.”
Territories of trash, compacted
by an invisible hand. Its gaze
is a laceration in the field
of sight. It punctures the cloud
of plastic that memory draws
across its objects. It displaces
the wound from eye to eye.
It already entails the production
of value. In this image,
the body is an unresolved incision.
Nothing is its neighborhood.

---

grammar

“Northwestern will now work with the City of Chicago and Ald. Brendan Reilly to move forward on the University’s plans to build a new, state-of-the-art biomedical research facility on that site. Doing so will create approximately 2,500 construction jobs, 2,000 full-time jobs, have an annual economic impact of nearly $400 million on the area and make Chicago a global leader in medical science.”

—“Statement on Dismissal”

fig. 11. Any house is a factory. Any house is a clock. Wait what about this. This house is dense in human mud. This house is a cellphone that doesn't hold its charge. Looking at it is a kind of love. A kind of language. In the workshop, someone said, "When language stops being clear, it stops being language." He did not want language to stop. Ok, but isn't there enough. I would not want

tough

"Northwestern has a proven record of commitment to preservation, which will continue. The historic buildings on Northwestern's Chicago campus designed by renowned architect James Gamble Rogers have been carefully maintained and renovated by the University for nearly a century. Northwestern University is committed to preservation and consistently wins historic preservation awards for the restoration and renovation of major buildings on its Evanston campus."
—"Finding Tomorrow's Cures"

---

luck

to endure. I would not want. As if I could stop. Each thing is full and replaced by the next thing: e.g., I buy a block of cheese then I buy another. When I put it in my mouth it makes me. Having some cash is like, I'm open to that. I'm down with that. Ok, but isn't there enough.

"The new building on the Prentice site will be connected on a floor-by-floor basis with the existing University research building just to the west of the site. Doing so will bring researchers together and thereby enhance the chances of finding breakthroughs in cardiovascular disease, cancer, diabetes and neurodegenerative disorders, among others. The site is the linchpin for what will be a major new medical research hub."

—"Statement on Dismissal"

fig. 12. **If I announce to a group of strangers that I am in pain. If I reach this ghostly position, a regiment of raw bottles, oozing mortar and form-marked concrete. If the lips of the wound are designed for excavation, Roses of shale, roses of shall, pressed into the carpet. If I recline in the corpse of the meadow to peruse a bridal magazine,**

"suppose these houses

are composed of ourselves"

then I came to a luxuriant city. Then I pealed back the surface of the river to show the bodies packed there. Then their gills, green from prolonged contact with chemical fertilizers. Their udders, chapped and tanned with antiquity. The men, draining the celestial liquor burdened within them. Then it roams the shady hills, swallowing the arbors and fog. Then it frames a space in which it lays a subdivision, a golf course, an Olive Garden.

**fig. 13. "I have had memories almost my entire life." The words of a student. As it is, abandonment fills her hand. Skirts
of ash, bed of smoke.
"Go to the dead and
love them," Creon says.
Then: "Everything should be
the result of a caress."
Nonetheless, he is an idea
being whipped. He is forcibly
fed with bitterness.
His wound becomes his pleasure.
That's enough about him.
Into the grave he goes.**

America isn't

"Northwestern will conduct a design competition for the new biomedical research facility. The University will invite many of the world's best architectural firms, including Chicago firms, with substantial accomplishments in designing biomedical research or similar buildings to submit expressions of interest and statements of qualifications."

—"Statement on Dismissal"

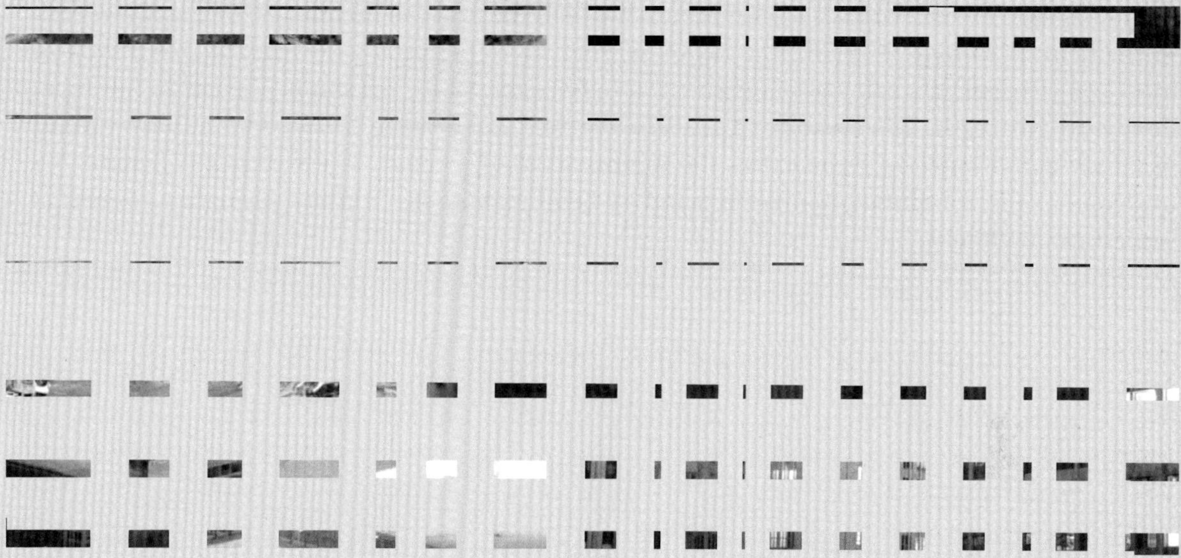

hard to see

What does the grave restrain?
A question for my students.
Not pleasure, but pain.
That's what they say.
They seek a world
beneath or beyond writing
whose weight is slowly
being removed.
"Poetry can be a beautiful place
to struggle." The words
of a friend. Groaned in a public
voice. But o my god
I am not content
until love itself prevails in art.
Much more than what I saw music.

fig. 14. **In the camera, you see a scar. Beneath which the grave is mobile, cutting soft trespass in the field. It cannot restrain. The action of your hand between your legs. In this way, you meet the weather, the color of concrete. You believe the whole person is present in her face. Tenderly sovereign. You treat her face as a scaffold for healing tissue. The minute tuning of an air conditioner as it measures the temperature of a room. The weather is fragile. No one can have it. A building resists the wind by bending with it. "But the strength to perish is sometimes withheld."**

one self

"The University will maintain its partnerships with the city and the Streeterville community on ways that Northwestern can continue to benefit both the neighborhood and the University's students, faculty and staff on our Chicago campus."
—"Statement on Dismissal"

---

is probably enough

You always leave a room when you know you're one hundred percent done with it. You love an injured place. The heart of the rotting tree. Patches of DDT on the lawn. Tomorrow is to mend. To mend instead of measure. To open the camera's aperture. To break the bonds of distance and death. Granary stars that mark the limits of safe navigation. In this way, writing is trespass, the sore through which the world passes. In this way, writing is corn and soybean seeds over which the earth has closed. Museum of the seam.

***No one can have it*: The photos in "Mandatory Fields" and "Bruise Smut" are screenshots from a YouTube video called "Prentice Women's Hospital Demolition Time Lapse," posted January 22, 2015 by the National Trust for Historic Preservation. In my submissions to magazines, I assured the editors that "the video is licensed under a creative commons attribution" which "allows for reuse." No need to worry. Everyone's property is clean. Meanwhile, I was applying to jobs and grants. I could not stop asking for money. Indeed, this book is an extended cover letter, a way to make myself attractive to money. Ok, ok, good grief. Now tell us something we don't know already.**

THE INSTITUTION AND ITS MOODS

"For oh, for oh

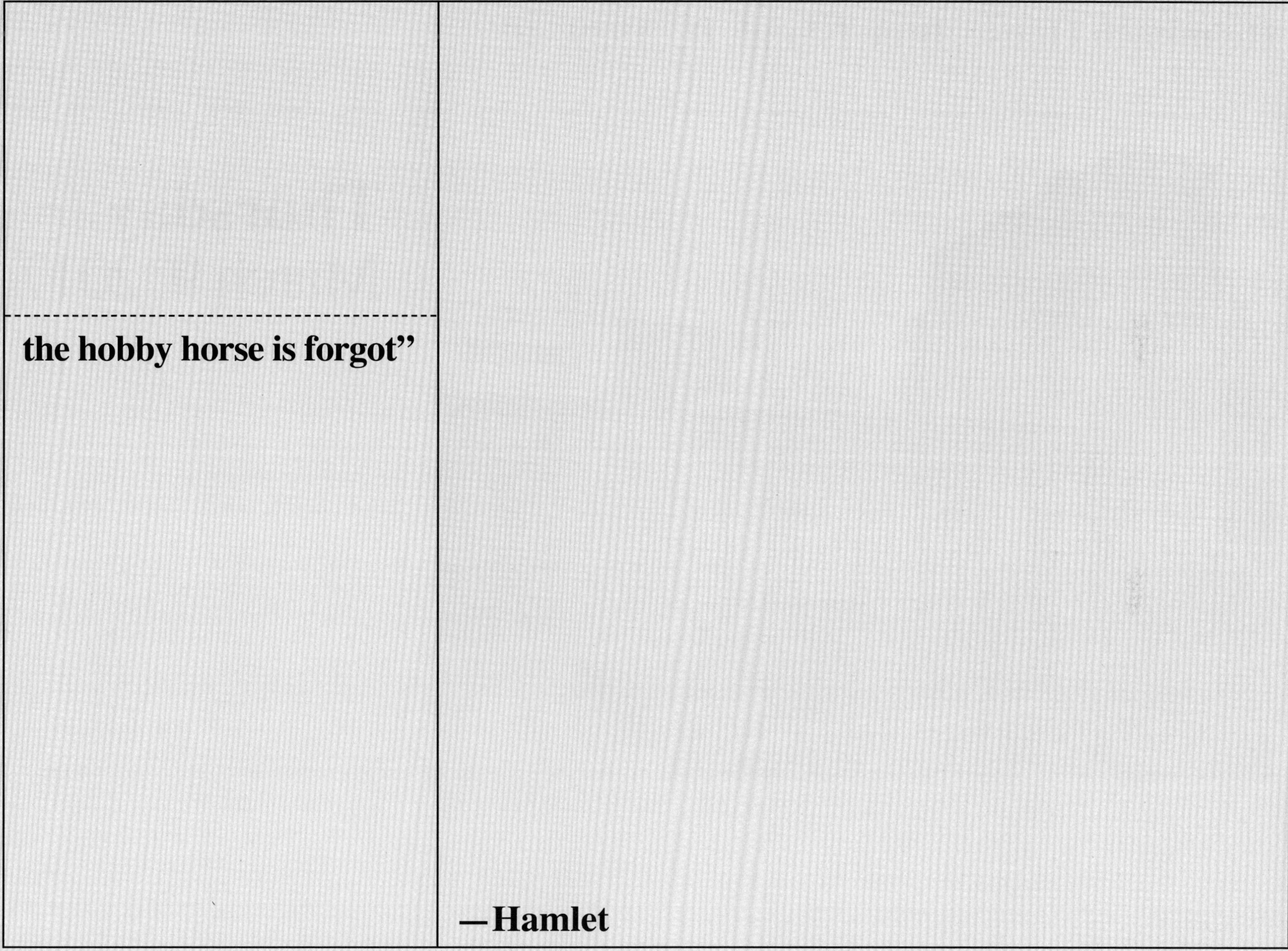
the hobby horse is forgot”
—Hamlet

Heimbach House, Blue Island, IL, 1939–40

fig. 1. the swerve in the curtain

Thursday
March 9, 2017

Even when it was standing, Prentice was somehow impossible to see. I deprived myself of its presence. I walked down Superior with my mom and I forgot to look up. Confession: I don't remember looking at it. Until it was demolished. And then I saw it through a lens: reducing the building to brittleness. So, I left my desk and went out to find Bertrand's other buildings. I pointed my iPhone at them and I wrote down exactly what I saw. I saw trash bags full of diapers and dog treats, shards of shatterproof glass. Is this the opening of thought, writing in public, alone, sweaty, carrying too much stuff? In March, I rode the L to a place called Blue Island to see the house he built for Dr. Aaron Heimbach, a country gent with an X-Ray machine in his front room. His syntax was division, to partition medical practice from the space where life—animal, ecstatic, bland—tries to last. Fat chance. "Viewed from the corner of the large lot, the Heimbach House reads as a series of disarticulated volumes and planes." Not a curtain, but a drain. A ladder into infinite space: ivy, mortar, money. Now his house is an annex to the police station across the street. Both buildings dressed in dark plains of durable brick, as if to model the prairie they burned or buried, borrowed or bought. How long will it be till the clouds take revenge on us? From the train, I saw a white man laughing in the closed precincts of his Nissan. Surely his house is full of plump towels and fresh linens, so that the closet is overflowing and he opens it carefully, conscious of collapse. And what is he but this ringing at Easter, knowing neither he nor I can last? Each of our actions taxes the future. The future is a blue island.

In his search
for meaning,
the chicken exhausted
all the resources
on his side
of the road.
That's the punch
line of a joke.
It's funny because
you expect
a better joke.
A lot of life is
what you expect it to be.
For instance,
I expect to be
wicked fresh
in the grave.
Howdy
to the speechless
dead. What a world
what a world
say the dead
so they're not
exactly
speechless but
possessed
by breath
from another place.
Crossing is
their bodies
now.

Drexel Home and Gardens, Chicago, IL, 1954–55

fig. 2. so remodeled that I'm not sure, even now, that I went to the right place.

"I became," Bertrand says, "sort of interested in another aspect of architecture: not interested in architecture as a series of individual projects . . . but to see how those various projects began to influence other peoples' lives, who weren't our clients necessarily." So, he scraped away half a block of Drexel Avenue and built these mathematical villas. Cubes of brick and cinderblock, built fast, below cost. He built to bring the city back, young and dense, better than it was before. For instance, these cinderblock huts were designed to be an integrated community. That's sweet, isn't it? Meanwhile, the banks refused mortgages to white families who wanted to move in. "They said that any white family who felt they could live next door to blacks was either crazy or liberal, and in either case, they weren't a good mortgage risk," Goldberg recalled in an oral history. "I can remember that quotation. It has stuck with me for all these years."

Wednesday
April 18, 2017

The mason who does clean work. The woman in sensible shoes walking to the bus, her hair unfurled by the wind. The carpenter who builds a casket in the morning, then sits on it to eat his lunch. You are not among them. You married within your class. You slept with men and women and most of them were white. Why does your life matter and why does it persist? You are the fragile white tissue of an almond bough around which the land collapses. A Swiffer wet wipe sweetens your trash. You are weary of the ancient and unkempt. Perfume where the dog slept.

When you were young, your mother took her friends to see Cabrini-Green. Turning on Division Street, she locked the doors of her Honda, ostentatiously. In this way, you learned that whiteness is a lash, a lock, a fortress on wheels, a burial plot. And who are you to ask for anything else, wrapped in the Patagonia she bought you, shocked by the sight of anyone? It's spring, you're writing behind a fence. In fact, you said, to no one, all white writing is writing behind a fence. And if you don't know that by now, you must wear the blue jersey of the police. You must be absolutely modern. Only the police are absolutely modern.

You have a strong work ethic. And you sometimes thank the police for their professionalism and diligence. You cross a picket line to enter an art museum with your date. Even when you are hungry, hungover, or sad, you continue to purchase and produce. You invoke the freshness of the bridal bed. Husbands in the twilight rain, one hand on the brim of their hats. Like you, they are sculpted to the demands of their desks. In their beds, the state is a legible text. Think of it as the word "dusk" projected on a dark screen. If you read it, you have to live in it. This radiant winter garden. This nickelodeon where emptiness unfurls from the hands of Moses (Robert). And how did you expect a young professional to stand in a place like this, making breakfast, censored or regulated in all her daily acts by the low slab of the roof, the beige siding her husband put up to give the building a human touch? At the cornice, a pack of black cables punctures the ceramic shell to bring the Internet in. Now the building is an edible Internet. Water follows through the cut.

Pineda Island, Spanish Fort, AL, 1956–60

fig. 3. I'm thinking, where does property come from, but I already know.

"My message," Bertrand said, "is much more important . . . than the quick identification as the round-building architect. I am talking about the performance of people in a social system, about the performance of people in the city." Be that as it may, he is remembered now for roundness, plump windows, pillows of concrete. And he learned to build in circles here: this middle-class resort named after a conquistador on an anonymous island in Mobile Bay. Formal, but not straight. Endless causeway, standing on delicate legs. The resort closed almost immediately due to what one website calls, euphemistically, "financial difficulties." Now you can find it only with GPS coordinates, moldering behind a fence. Posted. No trespassing. I respect a fence, I even love it. Down here everyone knows borders are hot. I asked Nick what to do in Mobile and he said, "Stay for the sunset, all the offshore rigs light up like crystal cities." Thanks, Nick: I see them now, lights of the future, diseased cattle, and impure butter, given that the law is light and light is labor.

In an old poem, I describe the arrival of a stranger. "We bought him a bag of sliders and fries," I wrote, "to pay the pleasure of dwelling." After he closed the window, his knuckles reeked of rosemary. The warp in a shelf of brick. He walked through the rain, begging for cigarettes. He abandoned the past or he caressed the narrow stem of a lamp. He spoke to the horses and the horses changed all our names to "Solomon." In a dream, I press my palms into the façade of his face. Who is gentle enough to love it? The faculty of his eyes drains into my fingers. They wither beneath the pressure, unaccustomed to tenderness. "The triumph of rot," he said, "by braiding it gently." I would say a kind of pregnancy. Like many men, I fantasized about being encumbered: beneath me or inside, weaving of a new body. Who is gentle enough to love it? In an old poem, the virgin, her luminous face, framed by roses. Dreamed she was whipped by angels. Lash of paint. Casket of butterflies. Open in the earth to receive her. Wild grass caressing the windows of her face. She lives embraced by green, embraced by glass. As if this world were not her home. As if this wound would be the last, beyond which, flowering command. Thus she speaks the language of broadband. "Southern light is future-proof fiber," she says. Her name is written in oil, heavy, adhesive, until it begins to smoke. Too often suffering from trash: her cattle at work in a field of garbage. She is entering a century of death. The traditional marks (Christ Victorious) have been replaced by terms like "Crisis" and "Debt." Stuffed with cotton or tobacco. The heat like a tight collar. Which means: memory overtakes you.

the present is
when i was saying

Monday
July 18, 2017

southern fiber
is future-proof light

Astor Tower, Chicago, IL, 1958–63

Astor Tower lifts off a shaft of exposed concrete. Not pictured. Twenty or thirty feet above, the building unfolds, a long rectangular volume. For use and habitation. Not pictured. The curtain wall is framed in semi-translucent blue glass, a porous boundary, through which the city can partially pass. Not pictured. Standing on the street corner beneath the building, I see in the lower windows a series of silk shades. Not pictured. The problem is: how to house the rich. North of Division. Proposition: the rightness of knife, the biting edge, the bare, repetitive box. Not pictured. Bertrand's building is a vertical grid, an extension of the street into the sky. What does a grid contain, he seems to ask. Persistent departure, thickness of grass gone to seed. Not pictured. To write about it is to figure the boundary, to put a finger on its limits and be repulsed. Elsewhere Bertrand revolts against such boxing and unboxing, the transport of merchandise in long, steel containers. Does he surrender here? As I walk the prosperous blocks around the building, my eye is drawn to the awning, long span of cantilevered concrete that extends from the building's core to the street: as if to assert the capacity of architecture to be the bridge which the city crosses, asthma freight, ashes, and leaves, ropes of electricity in a subterranean weave. Not pictured. Underneath the long tongue of the awning, Bertrand makes space for comment and complaint: silver light-buds framed by round aluminum disks. Why do they succor? They do.

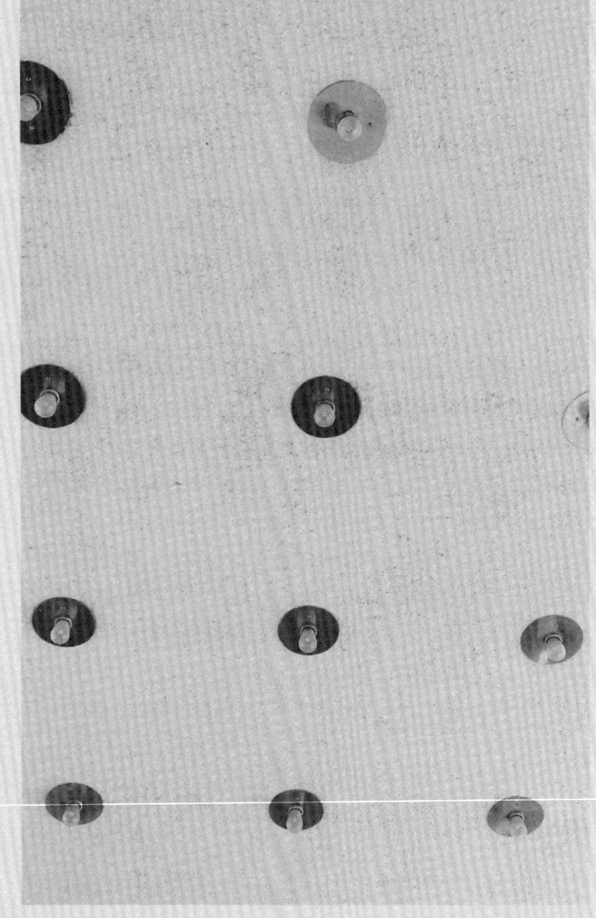

Wednesday
June 29, 2016

fig. 4. excluded from all the engines and doorjambs.

prose water			
crab tense			
	over the course		
	of its illness,		
	the building is		
	washed		
the cocked arm			
	of the scaffold	by the architect’s	hands
		working there	to produce
“Its essence is	ethical.”		
To expose structural	stone.		
Spanning without	softness.		
The cantilever and	the crutch.	bruised	fertilizer
To empty and clean	a colostomy bag.	muscle in	lather
		the dead man’s	vascular
		back	rift
		how can the	space
		architect	for
		open	it?

The man decides whether the man is superfluous. The street lamp deranges his geometry. Radiance. Clarity. Inclement copyright. A small dose of antidepressants to suppress hallucinations. It serves as a fortification. An industrial-sized box of Depends. A series of raw blocks. Wire grid. Pressure on the wound. To reduce it to light and volume. Edge and bruise. To make memory prosthetic. Prophylactic. Imperfectly stitched. To the thing it contains.

Marina City, Chicago, IL, 1959–67

fig. 5. Dazzled by June, I sit on the far bank of the river, across from Marina City. Behind me, bright scenes of commerce and prosperity: "Everything happens for a Riesling," a waiter's shirt announces. In front of me, a boy, maybe thirteen, drops his hook into the green darkness:

He caresses the river, as if to unwrap
tense pubic mullions, a kettle of silent
carp, their gills faintly flapping
in the river grass. His hook catches
and he wrestles up a red solo cup.
He makes a sign of embarrassment
and chagrin, this lamb who the police
closely kettle, this boy, bound
in blossoming muscle.
Then he sinks his hook again.
So too, the architect must advance
into the river, unbuckling, to crack
or caress the backbone crook of lime-
stone on which the city rests.
So too, he is undressed,
a strong man captured by sleep,
a man who built abundance.
"He is the joiner, he sees how they join."
He builds circular towers, flat discs,
spinal flutes that creak or flutter.
"Some loves are more failed than others."
His buildings crumple like a loose guitar.
He leaves a series of angles, Dick's Last Resort,
dew-wet, heavy, downcast,
as if to announce that luxuriance
is the property of heaven.
As if to say, the groin is where it splits
and becomes the heavy hull of a mid-sized car.
Beauty is addressed to no particular.

Thursday
June 30, 2016

fig. 5 (cont.). 1933. Le Corbusier and the fourth Congrès international d'architecture moderne leave Athens on an ocean liner. Behind them, Europe descends into black marble, leaves of beaten gold. Its combover capsizes in the storm. Absolved, they propose a clean, ideal city:

The architect shaves his flaky fingerprints
so that the pressure of his digits
leaves anonymous marks,
septic incisions
in the city's throat.
Madison: "The nation ought
to be constituted
to protect the minority of the opulent."
Ought to twist like a calf
caught in a barbed wire fence.
Its future is the asphalt artery
clotted with fallen brick.
It catches in the doorjamb,
or on the deck of a cruise ship.
It watches the world
windcracked, collapsed.
You will build
in quadrants and cuts.
You will divide
life into its constituents.
Each act will be clad
in concrete and glass.
You will build clean radiance,
a city in which the sutures melt
to leave cropped property,
a shimmering lot
of freshly washed rental cars,
bristle of rebar.
Each particular is addressed to beauty.

Astor Tower, Chicago, IL, 1958–63

The starving man becomes
his cloak, Manchester, Detroit, Shenzen:
melody of migration, melody of perishing,
sleeping beneath the viaduct or huddled in a door. His footstep triggers
unexploded ordinance
Yankee kindness
embroidered in the banks
of the Euphrates,

hypnotized by the pale unfolding powerpoint
many were the minds that capsized there
our boys in the almond groves

and the time they pass through
is heavy as crude

[black edge] [of insurance]
[embroidered] [in the bank]

[wallet of sandbags]
[to hold the river back]

"Be the bomb, see what it sees"

it is 10:45 am, Sunday
July 3rd, and Hilliard is
red expanse, vernacular flower,
that frames the security booth,

"Be the bomb, see what it sees"

trees without reticence, hot
charcoal in the grill,
freshly harvested hamburger,
packs of pink hot dogs,

"Be the bomb, see what it sees"

pink pacifier abandoned under a gate
low whistle of the L
and the grass itself
tough sudsy verminous

"Be the bomb, see what it sees"

defies the photographer's
impatience with things that are alive.

"[E]ven Mayor Daley, who visited the mock-up, declared that 'this is how people ought to live.'" "[T]he project . . . became distinguished over the years as the one building in the public housing system that did not need to be regularly policed." "While the three buildings—the Astor Tower Hotel, Marina City, and the Raymond Hilliard homes—were all high-rise residential buildings constructed of concrete, they exhibited notable differences in program, design and intent, not the least of which is that they were oriented to markedly different populations: a luxury clientele, the middle class, and lower-income families and senior citizens, *respectively*."

fig. 6. **"Plump stately Dick Daley."**
fig. 6. **"We're not happy til you're not happy."**

Sunday
July 3, 2016

Elgin State Hospital, Elgin, IL, 1965–67

1. In my dream, I see
a young white man
with a swastika tattooed
in the tender flesh
of his neck, smoking
next to a concrete mixer.
Prince of Blackwater,
what fracked pastures
are in his pockets?
Why does the daylight
embrace him?
His soldiers fire
biodegradable rounds
into the soft flank
of the burial mound.
What you see
is what you get:
the world like
a fractured lens.

2. For you were strangers in the land of Egypt,
for you traveled, easy as the dollar,
through subdivisions the color of dehydrated rose,
for you walked into the Fox River, fully clothed,
as though offering yourself for surgery,
river fed by highway brine and mercury,
and the river refused to open for you,
for you became your father, naked and bloody
in front of the camera, performing the murder
of your ancestors, for they refuse to enter the room:
to be a Jew in the twenty-first century is to be refused,
for the world you love is like a clouded iris,
for you built this world and your children rent it.

I walked long blocks of brick bungalows and I found myself at the headquarters of the highway patrol. I saw the suburb as though from the high cab of a police cruiser. I thought "I wish America were someone else's problem." The building is, as I feared, abandoned. A discarded place. In the hall, someone has dumped a steel rat trap, loops of black tube, a pile of shattered glass. As if to say, nothing here will be renewed. I take a picture of a winky-face, Gatorade blue, slapped at a jaunty angle on the window. I hide under the arch when the rain comes. Information, admission, security. Somehow the lawn remains plump: November green, ravished by the rain. Bertrand wanted to build a flexible city, compact, adaptable, contained in circular walls. He wanted to endow a space with nourishing. To leave a smear of honey on the counter at the bodega. "One always expects," Mendes da Rocha writes, "architecture to deliver extraordinary buildings which, however, change nothing whatsoever."

fig. 7. a building in a garden is a puncture in a garden.

Friday
November 18, 2016

Health Sciences Center, SUNY Stony Brook, NY, 1965–76

proposition: the present is whatever must be assuaged

I stand on the ambulance ramp and search for signs of ruin. A smear of masonry. The medical disk inside her ankle. Trampling tomatoes at the foot of the monolith. Poetry is sore concrete, fatigue in pre-cast sheets. The poet's task is to circle the megastructure, to measure it against the scale of seeing. The poet's task is to embrace a series of mundane acts. The disposal of needles. The harvest of marrow. The circulation of nurses. It is Monday morning, early, and their hair is wet from the shower. I am eating a hard, untoasted bagel in the hospital cafeteria so my appetite is still pretty much lawless. I am writing in public, rushing, putting things down as I think them, trying to resist the urge to check Facebook. "Poetry is the present written as the past," I write in my notebook: "the poet uses 'was' to describe her world because it already happened, because the world was naked and now it goes in thick robes."

I mean, for example, the way that lettuce is naked in the ground, but tightly fortified in its final fluorescent bath, gray aisles of the grocery. Allyson said that writing is a kind of contortion that produces legibility. She said she saw a bunch of helpful, attractive cops and we laughed. Thus lettuce is somehow godly: crisp, tasteless necklace of seed folded around an unnutritive essence. O pale heart of the plant, I recline in a communal garden beneath the heavy hospital. I regard concrete panels, dark columns of structural steel, daily diuresis. I endure rain, purple and gray. I study the limbs that join each tower to its twin. "This must be the worst hospital ever," says a woman with thick Long Island in her mouth. "LIFE: it's about always craving more," announces an ad for a casino. Ok, yeah, that's just plain true. Even if the earth refuses to sustain us. As, perhaps, it should.

fig. 8. On the ambulance ramp.

To write in public, as I am doing now, one must first surrender the idea of transcendence. That the poem is a disembodied hand. That it weaves or strokes a sheet of luminous plastic. Everywhere the poem goes it encounters devastation, or its seeds. While I sit beneath Bertrand's towers, two blond women groom the garden, a janitor pushes a garbage can, a student steps out for a smoke. They regard me with lawful suspicion. I leave with a sense of oncoming demolition. The buildings are badly maintained. They are not loved. How long can they possibly last?

Friday
August 1, 2016

St. Joseph's Hospital, Tacoma, WA, 1969–74

fig. 9. carbon rope

They are called—as if he built music—"The Goldberg Variations": six hospitals that fold and shiver, plastic curves, painted white to give them volume and gloss. Six hospitals and one is missing. Pictures do not show how sensuous they are, how the folds fold on each other as you walk around them: a body in the presence of a body. Pictures do not say how his buildings take the weather, smudged at the cornice, a ridge of shattered glass to keep the pigeons off. Built on a high hill in Tacoma, St. Joseph's stands like a flock of birds on narrow legs. It threatens to lift into another world, juicy place that Nixon cannot reach. Say that you want this world and it is yours. It hides inside of money. It is the low moan that currency makes against the world. It is the thought that makes your camera drunk. This building exalts the act of looking. It teaches you to see another world in the folds of this one.

A headache makes your mouth plunge, then it pulls away. The smell of diesel or the smell of rain. Now you are a thick suburb. Under the pressure of a credit card. Your body is a box of mirrors, a mercury mine. You have blossomed and spread, white mystery of spring. All your blood and treasure is spent. O rose, you are sick. The morning rain does not nourish you. Your mouth is caught in a rigid O. Where only deficit is at home. You stand beneath a white hospital, almost drunk. You cannot say why your sense is drenched: exhaustion or debt. What's the difference again? A braid of eyes. Curtains the color of a dove's wing. Ceramic lips framed against seismic shatter. "Soft zone." Meanwhile your uncle is dying in San Francisco and you do not know it. You are standing in front of another hospital whose patients are strangers. You unwind a rope of carbon so that you can post pictures of it on the Internet. How much damage does your life do and how can you refuse? O rose, you are sick. Only injury sustains you.

Sunday
April 30, 2017

St. Mary's Hospital, Milwaukee, WI, 1972–76

fig. 10. **"Every moment must destroy suffering anew"
—Alice Notley**

1.

Say you're building a table. At this table, it will be possible to eat an unremarkable meal. Or you might lay your taxes across it, many forms and receipts, since your jobs are brief. Say that the table is made of particleboard or plywood, something you pulled out of the neighbors' trash and laid across two sawhorses. To describe this table, you begin with experience itself. "How" (you are addressing an audience) (an audience under sedation or restraint), "does it cohere?" You quote a line of poetry

2.

Say you're invited to give a poetry reading in a bar or gallery. Instead of polishing and printing your poems, you find a sheet of blue linen, perhaps twenty feet long and thirty feet wide. You carefully punch holes in it, none more than an inch in diameter. You scrub it by hand, roughing the fibers. You wrap yourself in it at night, so that your sleep is embraced by blue folds.

“If architecture were considered speech,” Doug says, “then we would live in a very different world. Because it would be protected. You could build whatever you wanted.” You tried to imagine this world. You were almost frantic with imagining. You imagined cities waxy and wet. Buildings that take the shape of feeling or consume it, hungry for distress. Yet, you learned through hard experience that architecture works to secure silence, discretion. A hospital, if it is well-made, acts as a sealant or a border. It refuses to explain the nature of pain: to say the extent to which pain is not an exception to, but a condition of, the city around it. This is part of what makes Bertrand’s hospitals so strange. Their viscosity. Their intimacy with pleasure. They are unconcealed and they are not ashamed.

e.g., “being many, seeming one.” You wanted to build this object in such a way that it is free to have a life without you. You wanted it to unfold as a BUDGET unfolds. Tentacles of gray silk or chemical snow. And all the city is its organ. In its presence, you have no knowledge of what you are. Or this knowledge has no value to you.

Friday
November 10, 2017

You wear it under your clothes, so that it becomes intimate with your skin. Then when it is your turn to read, you unfold it, draping it over the audience. It hangs above them, suspended a foot above their heads. Under this altar, this veil, this cloud, you instruct them to walk into the street. They move as if they were one body. In the street, you ask them to look up. What do they see? They see a series of constellations, produced by the interactions between the punctures in the cloth and the street lights. They see a world without changes. Unhealing because unhurt. They see the goddess of love step out of the bath. Her body, as they see it, is a bent guitar. Her body is many voices breaking, separately, into song. They see you pliant, productive, and competitive. They admire the elegance of the vessel, the way you contain many mortgages. A sight so nourishing the BUDGET would buy it up.

Brigham and Women's Hospital, Boston, MA, 1976–80

I came to Boston with a lot of stuff. I meant to travel indefinitely. I wrote as though drugged, without purpose or direction. My body traveled without me. I looked fragile and fat. I said to my friends, "I am being devoured by the present." Run down by an SUV or looking for a place to pee, strangers trying to comfort me. Indeed, I am bereaved, the whole day is haunted by dying, by the names of my dead: Steven, John, Lori, John, dumb Yankees with their mouths painted shut. I would build a hospital for them, a house for the weary. I would build it out of tough country as Bertrand did at Brigham. A hospital so raw it seems to injure the city around it. Until every child is well, the dead do not ask for easy rest. Bertrand least of all, whose buildings are unwashed, untended, or demolished. At Brigham, he built a swerve, concrete pillars embraced by sensuous turns. When I visit, his burst of intoxication is constrained by an orange construction fence. As if to protect the city. From contagion. I lift my phone over the fence to get a picture of it (*fig. 11*). This is what the picture says: lay a mortgage on me. Repeat.

Monday
May 22, 2017

1.
You descend from a lovely place and the smell of barbeque follows you. Your sleep is more and more troubling. In a dream, you sit next to the architect, close enough to feel the progress of his breath, his legs, pressed together to suppress urination. He is retired and he lives in a leafy place. He is a green window. He tells you he's reading a book about love, then he tells you a story from it. In the dream, you are there for hours, time stretched like a thread of cement. When you wake the dog is whining in the next room. You do not remember anything he said.

2.
In another dream, you watch a dome of concrete explode, some brutal monument native to your mind. You have studied demolition: now your eye feasts on it, gift from the American wilderness. You dare to say that you are a person with dark and sometimes questionable values. You want to pay to make it beautiful. Ok. Lay a mortgage on me. Repeat.

3.
All forms of demolition are native to your mind. Last night, you lay on a yellow hill and the hospital was almost inside you, a cream beyond its lawns. Then you saw the bismol frothing at the root. All its acres are nauseous and untuned. You are its true landlord. Even in sleep, the future pursues you.

4.
The BUDGET is designed to confuse your body. Your body is confused: patrolled by parties of ravenous grooms. How celibate you've become, how dedicated to the BUDGET. You fortify your mortgage or a mortgage fortifies you. Each day you forget a song you love—the words or the tune. Hold on. Let me try to sing it back to you.

You dare to say. Quoted from Goldberg's 1964 lecture, "The City Within a City." Like much of Goldberg's writing the talk assails the rote formalism of the so-called "International Style," with its preference for razor-sharp boxes, steel, and glass, raw majesty of industry. Elsewhere in his notes he writes, "The box: 1. A uniform for the uniform. . . . 2. Container without content." A box denies or suppresses the task of architecture: to make a space for manyness and intermingling, the unplanned crossing that characterizes human community. "Space for living—space for changing and space for movement." Space for dark value that exceeds our capacity to speak it.

Good Samaritan Hospital, Phoenix, AZ, 1978–82

"You are going on a journey," a stranger whispers in your ear. His face is painted with thick shadow to preserve his privacy, but his voice is subterranean. "And on the way, you will burn a bucket of oil and breathe the fumes, wafting them toward you with a turn of your wrist, so that green visions descend on your house. Your life is sustained by small pleasures you cannot afford. You make the city easy. To leave." Lifted from your mother's desk, where you were writing a book called *The Institution and Its Moods*, you are, without warning, going on a journey you cannot afford, bright threads of oil burning before you. And your head and your hands are wreathed in petroleum smoke. Green visions descend upon you. In the first vision, you are standing in a crowd of corpses. They appear as angels, worms, nixes, chimera, sphinxes, or disembodied hair. They carry a bundle of tobacco or they glean chaff from a shattered field. They are fetching water or they are elbow deep in linen, intimate with detergent and laundry, other warm commodities. You are among them, married and prosperous, lounging in the gate on your way to Phoenix. You are breaking the ice or you are showing off your genitals. You are sleeping in a mass grave, excavated by the city. The grave is beautiful, apportioned with golf courses and fountains. While you are walking through it, admiring the delicacy of the place, the BUDGET appears before you, white phosphorous blossoming in his larynx. He chews a mint placebo or he sucks a globe of Texas crude. He lays you on the back seat of his Buick, very gentle, and serves you a plate of cinders and cocktail wieners. You are stretched to the thinness of a dollar by his diet. You watch a photograph breed in your belly. What does the photograph show? It shows the BUDGET. You can smell a roadblock brewing in your arteries. Now the BUDGET appears within you as a blanket of ozone. The dead cannot rise through it. What evil humors lock and load tonight! Now you live in a world without exit. You are lying on a bed of grass. "Look," says a stranger's voice, "Even the ceiling is made of money."

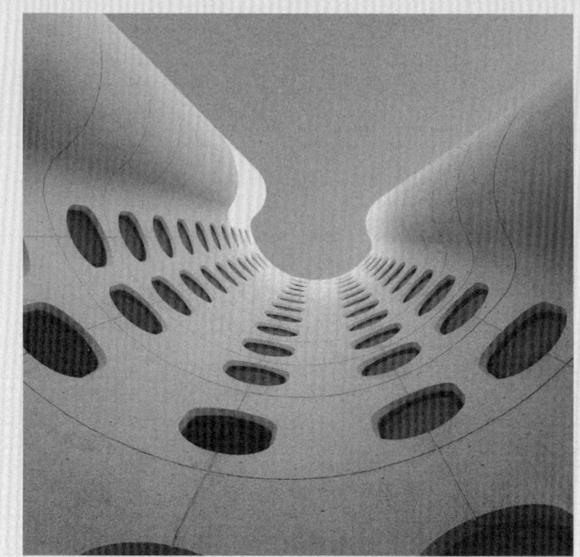

fig. 12. having banished the automobile and the academy,

Saturday

April 29, 2017

fig. 12 (cont.). having made gladness mandatory.

People, almost / ghostly / standing in the place / beneath / border between / the living and / the dead / red smudge / or dark rim / where the highway cut / their brows / releasing / the fragrance / of juniper / unwashed desert. / In the second vision, I am among them / wiping their brows / with a cool cloth / (though I am also / wounded) / (though I too / was caressed / by the BUDGET). / And the BUDGET / is among us / a newborn / at her breast. / And she and her child / are dead / blueshards of bone / piece their skin / And I wash / her face / the face of her / babe (here / no one / will be / refused) / I / anoint the bruise / beneath her jaw / so her voice / unfolds. / She caresses me / braiding and unbraiding / our fingers / and leads me forward / into a white hospital / O if a white place belonged / to anyone! / The patients there / are drunk with pleasure. / They give themselves / openly / a perfume of spice / and honey / heavy / in their hair, / their bodies / the consistency / of soft cheese / so that any of their surfaces / might open / suddenly / eager / to be fucked / and I slip / my iPhone / into one of them / so it can reach / this far shore / utopian breach / before me / Then / we are standing / on the steps / of a hospital / emaciated shades / our eyes / are pale / from long months / in the morgue. / Behind us / the hospital is / heroic / folding / almost liquid / not built but / spread by a knife / into this patch / of desert / 77 degrees in April / and I / am wearing / black pants. / It seems / some air-conditioned / shard / of the past / sweetened / by sheets of sandstone and / smooth-jazz / framed by succulents / the sun / like a slice of pale / melon / how light the BUDGET / becomes / undressed, / is the body / of a dove / unafflicted by capital / and having no / privacy / in its patriotic / place / though a power / of property / still works / (a body / is not / yet / held in common). / Until / it is / death / is the only news / how much / and / how soon. / And until / it is / the sheriff / of Maricopa county / haunts the birth room / speaks / a language / of smiles / and the BUDGET / is exhausted / she casts her vote / for the party / of misery / she needs / a place / to rest / any white / place / will do.

Providence Hospital, Mobile, AL, 1982–87

fig. 13. "the load-bearing walls–are so thin that the contractor at first doubted they could be built as designed."

Careful to exclude the faces of patients and ambulance staff, I try to photograph it and mostly fail. No one here likes me. In turn, I am not easy: anxious, as always, to say a lot. As if these poems could be complete: a record of a world that has nothing but needs. It survives, precisely, on the price of insurance. It requires gouged bodies, burnt bodies, torn. Handguns that backfire, bursting the barrel. It has been, as usual, redecorated without taste. To signal the building's submission to illness. I grow weary describing it. How many pale chapels. How much cement. Oh great, another hospital. Why did he build so many? And why did he build so much the same? There was nothing else for him to do. He sought the immensity beyond which a building becomes a living thing. He sought the dollars to make his buildings live. But the BUDGET withdrew from him. So what. The BUDGET loves none of us. What he built is just a screen or veil beyond which a bright underwater city waits, where

Sunday
July 17, 2017

As you return from sleep, the smell of cotton, pralines, salted fish. Like the memory of a lovely drug that turned your stomach once. You thought you were traveling into a kiss. You thought you lay on the anatomist's table, gently unfolded by his knife. You were saying how thin a city can be, and how damp. Who knows what you meant. Slow down, slow down. No one has invented aspirin yet. Your love is a complicated wage, but it keeps the headache (barely) away.

the patients are lifted from their beds and taken into blue mystery, breathing easy in the deep, their cancers cured and their bones unbroken, their bodies undressed or stretched, long flagellates that pierce the pores within the BUDGET. Where they travel, no one can say. Perhaps into Mobile Bay. And how long until the bay marches up the hill and kisses us, fed by glacial run off, so that nothing here remains? Nothing personal anyway.

Didn't you live a patriot's life? Isn't your safe word *debt*? Thank you for choosing Providence. If you have a memory, you probably need it. Badly. For instance, I remember undressing as an adolescent. What is your substance and whereof are you made, I would say, turning my palms up in a gesture of deference. Or I would say: Dear Toby, your body is wrong. Signed, your unhappy customers.

River City II, Chicago, IL, 1983–86

Crisp squares of concrete, the brain in a bath of glass. It fills with the smell of fennel. Like cold water or a kiss. I'm standing in the kitchen and obviously it's raining blue swoon of the branches, twilight like a low throat. Meanwhile, she rubs a hole in her delicates. Tedious thatching. A place of spores and spokes. How pleasure makes fluid derelict. To produce through light alone. To manage anxiety by provoking it in small doses. To feel anything? No, to feel what. Arose instead of rose.

---

coffin

"Act so there is no use in a center." Act so there is no use in a rose. Heap up the fabric of the sentence. Say the names of flowering shrubs. Write as though you are holding up a heavy bag or bottle. The tired arm of language. The exhaustion of the thing it describes. Nothing is lost on you. Nothing lets you be lost.

Sunday
July 3, 2016

All afternoon, I read about Bertrand's final years: his failing practice, buildings designed but never built. He tried to make the city a place of density and pleasure. To score the daily paths and purchases of human life. He wanted to build an architecture for loneliness. An architecture for need. It somehow escapes the capacity to be seen. At River City, for instance, he could finance only a twelfth of his design, despite investing his own capital in the project, tempting failure and collapse, the loss of his practice. Even so, River City seems badly maintained and underused. When I visited it in the summer of 2016, its plateaus and plazas were populated by weeds and standing water. The neighborhood around it is a glue trap for young cash. A city is like an ancient star, which accumulates mass and density as it ages, Bertrand said. Implying, of course, that it is indiscriminate gravity, that it swallows whatever falls into its orbit. It does not ask if there should be living. It simply feeds on life. He died without sycophants. He died without history. "We can build whatever we can think," he liked to say. Should we?

AFTERWARDS

“Thus did I strangely war

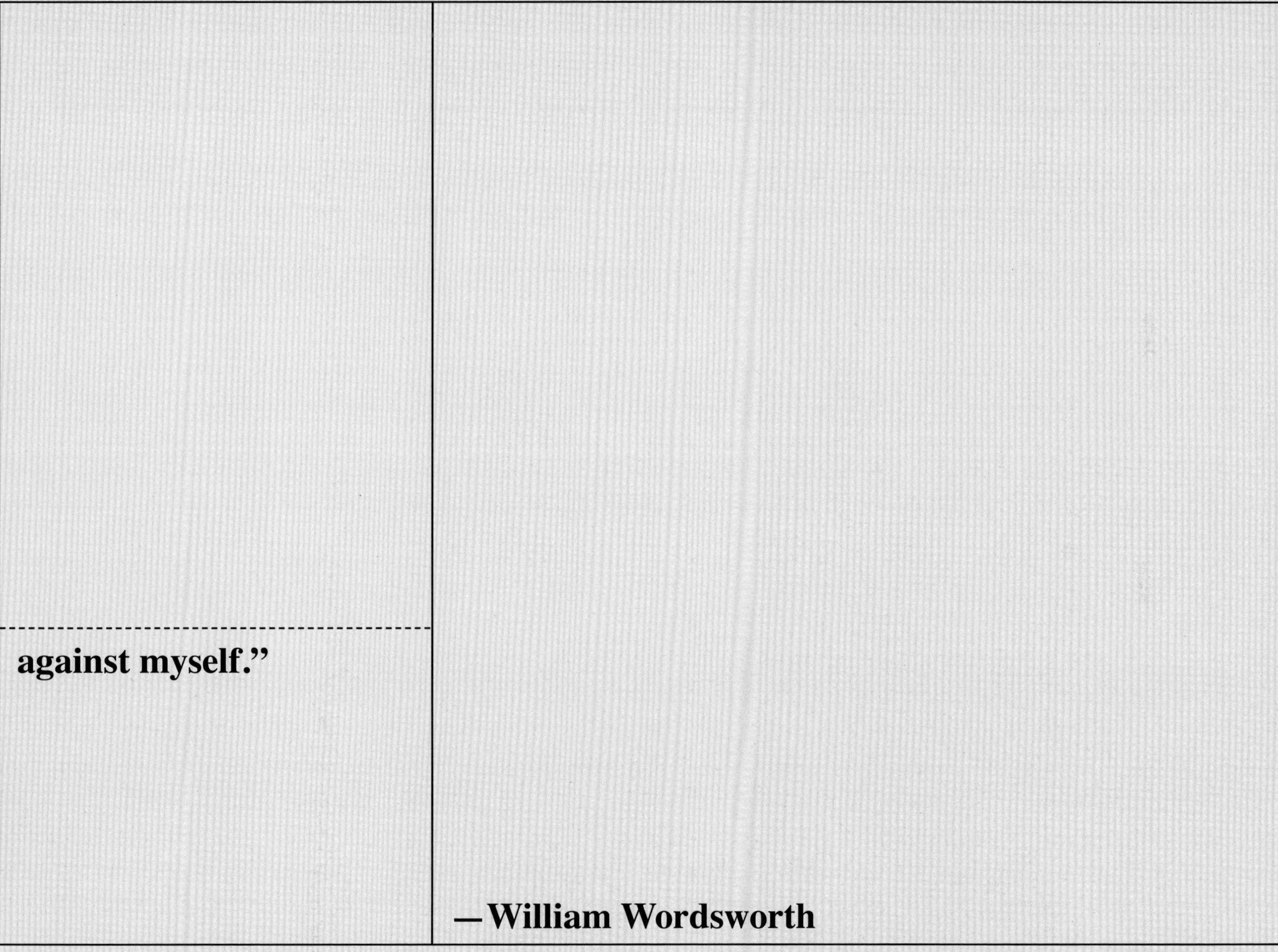

against myself."

—William Wordsworth

I thought I was done with this book. I stopped writing it at the end of 2017. I was living in Iowa City. I had just moved there. It is the end of 2019 as I write this afterword. I am living in a new city: Denver. I text Liana and tell her that Denver is like an "engorged Chipotle." All the men in their sleek Patagonia jackets. One would call them "sporty." They are up early with their bright-eyed, bouncy dogs. They are lounging in the park, beneath which there are many paupers lying in cheap wooden coffins. To be surrounded by strangers, their large happy animals. To have no part in that happiness.

It is the end of 2019. I find myself aching. In response to some absence or incompleteness. The ache, which is a kind of delay. A puncture in a brick wall. And the day is closing around me. I find myself turning backward: rehearsing the trips I took to see Goldberg's buildings. The experience of traveling, alone, on an inexplicable errand. I found myself wandering around strange cities, looking for places to shit. At Sea-Tac, in April 2017, I walked a long way around the airport, its ramps and turns, to find my motel, the Rodeway Inn. Then, after four hours of sleep, the attendant at the front desk, insisted—again and again—that I had shared my room, that I did not sleep alone. Accusing me, I think, of hiring someone's company. Why else would I sleep in this margin of the highway? Why else this lonely figure in a strange city? Being to him, the attendant, illegible—except as a john. This was the last morning of my uncle's life and I spent it alone, in a strange city, trying to explain myself to strangers.

In other words, there is something inexplicable about this book, even to its author. Why, with the present escalating, terminally, did I turn with such obsessive fervor to a single building, a single act of institutional violence? I have tried to justify this decision, itself terminal, in cover letters—even in the text of the book—by describing the demolition of Prentice as an "allegory of neoliberalism." I may even believe this to be true. Yet, it is obviously insufficient to explain this artifact, this creature that I have lovingly sculpted over many years. At its heart, this is not a book about political economy or institutional critique. No. This book is about love.

I have some questions about that. What does it mean to love a building? Why do I do that? How does an object hold the eye, passing through it to engrave its image on the heart? Shakespeare: "mine eye hath play'd the painter and stell'd / Thy beauty's form in the table of my heart." Stell: to fix in position. To equip or dress with weapons. If I knew the answer, I would surely tell you.

The first Brutalist building, L'Unité d'habitation, was built in Marseilles, between 1945 and 1952. Before the war, its author, Le Corbusier, developed an architecture of uncanny smoothness and luminosity. He raised his buildings on concrete piers, *pilotis*, so they did not intersect with the earth. He hired contractors to paint and plaster over the rough surfaces of his concrete, "lavishing on it skilled labor and specialized equipment beyond anything the economics of the building industry normally permitted," as Reyner Banham writes in an ecstatic tribute to the new architecture. His writing is like that. Ecstatic, celebratory, seduced by the object it describes.

Le Corbusier's prewar buildings are an expression of faith in the power of the machine over the material. The architect's capacity to impose, to transform. To resolve, to smooth. The rough surface of human life. Architect Kengo Kuma reports that, in his *Œuvres complètes*, Le Corbusier even painted over the shadows in photographs of his buildings: "to create the impression of perfectly white walls . . . to expunge all textures." So that a building becomes perfectly visible. So that it is divided from the world in which it resides. Not an organ of the world but an *object*. That's what Kuma calls it: to say the way it is limited, fortified, defined by its borders.

After the war, Corbu turned away. His buildings become rough, unfinished: the unskilled local craftsmen, "whose carpentry rarely attained the level of precision required in the construction of a garden fence," left the concrete uncooked, the grain of the wooden formwork imprinted in it. Texture returns to his architecture, shadow. One must understand it as an attempt. However belated. To reckon with machines, their capacity for killing. To register that capacity in the material of a building, its cladding—so that, looking at it, one sees violence, catastrophe, the crack in the skull of the world. That indestructible trace which travels through the machine and returns into the figure who uses it.

L'Unité was designed as a solution to the postwar housing crisis: habitation made cheap, unfussy, quick. Now it is a pricey condo building in a leafy, bourgeois neighborhood. Complete with a boutique hotel, Hotel Le Corbusier. My wife and I stayed there for a night on our honeymoon. We stole a bar of soap as a souvenir.

The building, which is not only raw, but brutal: an expression of despair and fatigue. That despair, that exhaustion of human possibility: it turns out to be easy to live with—a good real estate investment. Even with their frayed surfaces, they remain complete and contained—a set of objects, that resist the ground on which they stand. And brutalism itself has become a lifestyle brand. The rough concrete, reproduced in the pages of glossy black-and-white coffee table books. In this way it demonstrates itself, inadvertently. It says: there is no violence—and no meditation on violence—that cannot be claimed as an aesthetic. A pricey aesthetic. Kuma: "How then can architecture be made to disappear?"

I thought I was done with this book. Yet, I find myself aching. A sympathetic response to something incomplete, unfinished. It is the end of 2019. I am living in a strange city and the day is closing around me. I write in scraps of time I steal from my freelance job—a job in which I paraphrase famous poems for high school students. *Bright light in the sky, I want to be as steady and stable as you are*. I write: *I can hear all of America singing: I hear the many different songs that people sing*. I apply for many jobs. When prompted, I affirm, "I am not a protected veteran." I write in my notebook:

> **I take it as a given**
> **that my body seeks**
> **its own extinction.**
> **To dissolve**
> **as compost dissolves**
> **into pungent, vegetable**
> **waste, where**
> **grubs and maggots**
> **make their pasture.**

This ache, which is the book I wrote. This book which is—has—the architecture of the ache. At first, I imagined it in four parts, fourteen sections each. Prentice had four wings, fourteen floors. The book, as I have it now, has three parts, with fourteen sections each. A wing is missing. I wanted the book to be the building. Then I didn't want that at all. I came to imagine the book as a wounded technology, a technology of incompleteness. *A constantly proliferating knot.*

As a young man, Bertrand Goldberg studied at the Bauhaus. This was in Dessau in 1932, 1933. The young Jewish architect, son of a bricklayer, forced to flee when the Nazis came to power. His body retreated: his art did not. He remained, for the rest of his life, committed to the ideals of the institution he fled. The aspirations of an extinct institution. Convinced that design could, through cheap, ubiquitous materials, make human life more bearable. Goldberg, 1974: "A new space can shelter a new life." Wagering that concrete or plywood might serve as the entrails of the world. From which, great loathing, great joy, depending on the season: in either case, the urge to make again.

In an important sense, Goldberg can claim vindication in this belief. His buildings were unusually active in the world. Marina City, for example. To fund the building, Goldberg convinced the Federal Housing Administration to change its definition of the family, recognizing, legally, for the first time, single-parent households as families. There is a waft of frankincense about it. I mean, it is kind of remarkable, given the moment: the late 1950s, the Midwest, the family as a sanctified instrument of the American state.

Remarkable too, given the prevailing theories of city planning. In 1933, Le Corbusier and a team of like-minded modernists abandoned the continent, setting out on an ocean liner from Athens to Marseilles. Over the course of the trip, they laid out a foundational vision for the modern city—the "radiant city"—organized into discrete, segregated zones. A place for living. A hive of office towers. Luxuries and shops. Separated by medians of grass. Joined by the automobile. So that the city digests any act to its perfect, distinct, radiant practice. And the life within it becomes as smooth as milk, and as contained.

At Marina City, Goldberg built against this precise and painful radiance. He enacts a dizzying impaction of functions. The iconic corncob towers press against a theater, an office building, an ice skating rink, a steakhouse named, improbably, "Dick's Last Resort," and a series of docks. All in the space of a tight half block. It becomes impossible to see in its entirety. Its relation to the city around it is complex, undecidable, invasive, and caressing. Beyond what an object can sustain. Like the great cities of history with their flows of cash, crops, ceramics, false prophets, quarters of meat, counterfeit currency, and secret police. Like history itself. Kuma: "While time can be rendered abstract in the framework of architecture, one cannot ignore time within a garden."

Goldberg was not a Brutalist. He built in concrete, yes. Unsmoothed concrete, with the grain of the wooden forms legible in its surface. He built as Brutalists do. But, unlike Le Corbusier, he never lost his faith in the capacity of design to remake the world. He built in cheap, ubiquitous materials because it seemed utopian to do so.

It feels bad. I know that. I mean, it feels bad to love these buildings. To look at them, to walk around them, watching them fold and unfold. They are fragments of another, better world, transplants that coexist uneasily, at best, with our own. There is something uncanny—untimely—about Goldberg's buildings. They seem alien and impossible. Impossibly joyous. *A constantly proliferating knot.*

The phrase is Georges Didi-Huberman's, describing the Laocoön. That mass of ancient travertine in which the human form wrestles to free itself from death. Reduced in this struggle to its fundaments: breath and muscle. The marble seemingly charged with motion: even in photographs, one sees its resistance. To being still. "A material capable of every type of metamorphosis."

This book does not end with presence, the fullness of Goldberg's realized vision. It ends with absence, the failure of memory. The author of these poems, struggling with the past. To struggle with the past being, in some sense, the condition of poetry: a science with no name. A science which is after dusk and out of doors. In the blue heat, sweating. In this way, the past begins to consume the present. Reduced to its fundamentals: matter and breath. Memory, which is analytic, which dissolves the world around it.

To struggle with the past being, in some sense, the condition of love. It is 2019. My uncle has been dead two years. He died alone, in a facility in San Francisco. I should've been there: I was supposed to be there. Instead, I was in Tacoma, photographing a Goldberg building. I thought I would stop off, make a little detour on the way.

It wouldn't be fair to say, exactly, that he killed himself. But he did destroy the vessel in which he lived with slow persistence and accuracy, sustained over many years. He was an

alcoholic and a dedicated pothead. Cocaine too, early on. In his twenties, he went to rehab, where, he later told me, he got his sense of smell back. He was a huge pain in the ass. When his father, the elegant surgeon, died, he flew into Chicago from San Francisco for the memorial; I drove to O'Hare to pick him up. My uncle would not come out, would not leave the airport. He stood at the bar drinking twenty dollar Budweisers while I drove in circles, looking for him. He was a pain the ass, but I loved him fiercely and forgave him always. He didn't have to ask. There was something broken, something that broke and failed to heal. Somehow a wound opened between him and the world—nothing could make it close.

I thought I was done with this book. I typed up my notes then I abandoned them. I discretely suppressed this text. I wanted to make this writing more incomplete. The question being whether, in service of incompletion, I should refrain from writing or continue to write. I inaugurated a series of other projects. It was a habit of the time, the production of fragments. Kuma: "No particular skill or effort is required to turn something into an object. Preventing a thing from becoming an object is a far more difficult task." Empty, impossible, the artifacts of my culture, which are, entirely, oil.

Somehow, my writing was not empty enough. It is 2020. I walk my ancient dog across the pauper's graves. I have returned, again, to this gesture: speaking after. It is a kind of speech that opens—then refuses—the possibility of closure. It is 2022. While my editors wait for a finished text, I am once again not writing this essay. A discipline of refusal, a science that refrains. Huberman: "history stirs. It moves, it differs from itself . . . Fluid in one place, but hard and sharp in another; serpentine here, but rock-like over there." If one is to resist the production of objects—in literature as much as architecture—one must produce a writing that fails. Fails to end. Fails to set, to harden in its formwork. A writing that has the bitter texture of history: biting, angular, precise, luxurious. It remains in motion even after its motion has ceased.

I wanted the book to become an aggregate instead of an object. A compound substance, sedimentary. I wanted my writing to take on the quality of concrete, the undigested sediment carried within it. Its difference, its resistance, giving the structure strength. And concrete is resolutely local—

creamy and soft, brittle and drab,
depending on the conditions
of the surrounding soil,

the research for this book being itself occasional and local. It carries as gravel carries: a heavy cargo of quoted, appropriated, imitated, and deranged language.

I make no apology for that and no accounting. I took the books that happened to fall into my hands: Claudia Rankine's *Don't Let Me Be Lonely*, Anne Boyer's *Garments Against Women*. In December 2013, with a bad case of the flu, I went to New Orleans to read with Laura Goldstein. I don't know why—I hadn't started writing or even imagined this discipline—but I bought a copy of *Clog Magazine: Brutalism* at a bookstore in the Bywater. Later, Laura's line—"be the bomb, see what it sees"—from *Safe Wars* became part of me. I heard it wherever I went.

I took what happened and I let it fall. When I went to Mobile, Nick Strum told me to look for the crystal rigging of the offshore oil platforms. I looked but I didn't see them. Harris Feinsod sent me an email about the abandoned hospital where Hilary Clinton was born. Allyson Paty said a funny thing about the cops. I was in New York, then, to visit the site of a building Goldberg didn't build, the ABC Tower at 67th and Columbus in Manhattan. "In photos, the model / of ABC tower is lit from within. / So that the news is / luminous. So that the building is,

a wick which descends
into undisclosed snickers
and twix. Body petroleum.
Whether it has a soul. Or not.

I wrote that, then I left. My hard drive is full of poems like that. From visits I made to see Goldberg's papers at the Ryerson and Burnham Libraries at the Art Institute of Chicago. From trips I took to see minor Goldberg sites. "Elsewhere is a negative mirror," Italo Calvino writes. And Heidegger: "What threatens is nowhere." Zoë Ryan's *Bertrand Goldberg: Architecture of Invention* guided me there. I carried it all over the country as I visited Goldberg's buildings, and I referred to it as a liturgical text. So too, Igor Marjanović and Katerina Rüedi Ray's *Marina City: Bertrand Goldberg's Urban Vision*—which taught me to see the activity of Goldberg's buildings, the way they shaped the world.

There are other books that shaped me. It is one of the pleasures of writing. The way that, working, obsessively, on a single theme, books find their way toward you, so that it becomes impossible to say how much of your substance resides within them. Hence, the futility of citation. You become a scattered, unsolid thing. Breathing—but through many lungs. It is the ongoingness of such scattering that I sing. Even in the final months of working on this book, news continued to reach me. Corinne Butta gave me Kengo Kuma's *Anti-Object*, which helped me think the object—architectural or literary. Thus, waiting for the train to ride to New York and see the place where the ABC tower would've been, I wrote in my notebook: *I have often sought gray unfolding: fog in the lap of the mountain.*

In his studies for the ABC tower, Goldberg discovered that the company was, in fact, many companies, organized into discrete pockets of purpose and activity. His design tried to amplify those organic connections by clustering the standard functions and spatial requirements of an office tower into petal-shaped pods that radiated from a central core. Each unit of the building, discrete, protected, yet joined to a whole.

ABC rejected Goldberg's design because, they worried, it would be difficult to sell. There was a kind of precision and intimacy in his practice that exceeds—disrupts—what capitalism asks of architecture. Where capital is concerned, a building is an empty box, pliable and mute.

There was a warning in this incident—of the fate his buildings would later suffer. Northwestern, advocating for the demolition of Prentice, argued that the building would be impossible to adapt to new uses. Too precise and too intimate with its original circumstances. The university's press releases from the period make this argument with energetic monotony. From an undated release, circa 2013: "Renovating the old Prentice Hospital building on Northwestern University's Chicago campus for use as a medical research facility is not feasible, according to a consultant's study." When the dead speak, many mouths drought.
In "Bruise Smut," I quote from Northwestern's press releases: documents in which officials—for instance, the cheerfully named bureaucrat Eugene S. Sunshine—make their case

for demolition and celebrate their victories over preservationists. As an employee of the university, these releases appeared unbidden in my email inbox at odd hours for several years. Then the building was gone and they stopped.

Standing at the corner of 67th and Columbus, beneath a building that Goldberg did not build—a building that, as Elizabeth A. T. Smith writes, "if built, would have without question changed the direction of Goldberg's practice and situated him more firmly and prominently as one of the major figures of his generation"—I wrote:

> No one asks
> where they've been.
> They are received with embracing
> joy. Their silence is the silence
> inside music.
> Only music interrupts it.

Goldberg was right: architecture can "shelter a new life." And when one compares him against today's starchitects, one feels the absence of his vision, his optimism, his commitment to the avant-garde as a site of collective betterment. One feels it as ache, fatigue, failure. He was right. He just wasn't right enough.

Goldberg is a failed figure—a figure of failure. He hoped his buildings would make life under capitalism more bearable, more human. They did not. But Goldberg's failure reflects. It has the luminous silver of a mirror. And the boundaries, the frame, the limits. The avant-garde of his period, and mine, haunted by its limits, its incapacity to drive meaningful political change. Take his buildings, then, as a cry: of exuberant anguish. A demand for another world. If this book joins his cry, extends it, offers it to the present, it also joins his failure.

ACKNOWLEDGMENTS

Poems from this book have previously appeared, often in significantly different versions, in the following journals: *The Atlas Review, The Black Warrior Review*, *The Colorado Review*, *Dreginald*, *The Journal Petra*, *Jubilat*, *Lana Turner*, *Poetry Northwest*, *Tagvverk*, and *Washington Square.* A poem from this book was featured on the PoetryNow podcast and later appeared on the Poetry Foundation's website. Several poems appear in a chapbook, *Every Hospital by Bertrand Goldberg (Except One)*, which was selected for the 2018 Ghost Proposal Chapbook Prize.

My abiding gratitude to the friends who read pieces and parts of this manuscript in various stages and offered their advice and encouragement: Emily Barton Altman, Janelle Effiwatt, Joseph Emanuel, Dana Fang, Emma Heldman, Micky Hill, Kamden Hilliard, Stephen Ira, Mike Lala, Iris McCloughan, Bianca Rae Messinger, Alyssa Moore, Allyson Paty, David Pritchard, Kristen Steenbeeke, Tasia Trevino, and Stella Wong. And to Wendy's Subway—particularly Corinne Butta, Xavi Danto, Rissa Hochberger, Juwon Jun, and Rachel Valinsky—who gave this book its architecture.

I did key work on this project during a residency at the Millay Colony in the summer of 2016. I also owe a great deal to a series of classes and workshops I took between the summer of 2015 and the fall of 2017 led (separately) by Simone Forti, Sueyeun Juliette Lee, Eileen Myles, D.A. Powell, and Elizabeth Willis. My thanks to all of them—they cleared the space where I try to stand.

Discipline Park

Passage Series #4
First Edition, 2023
Edition of 1,000 copies
ISBN: 978-1-7359242-8-1
Library of Congress Control Number: 2022946751

Edited by Corinne Butta
Proofreading by Juwon Jun and Rachel Valinsky
Design by Rissa Hochberger and Toby Altman
Typeset in Times
Printed at Ofset, Turkey

Published by Wendy's Subway
379 Bushwick Avenue
Brooklyn, NY 11206
wendyssubway.com

Wendy's Subway is a non-profit reading room, writing space, and independent publisher located in Brooklyn.

The Passage Series publishes titles by emerging writers and artists whose work manifests in innovative, hybrid, and cross-genre forms that imagine new possibilities and expressions of the poetic, the political, and the social.

***Discipline Park* was selected for the 2020 Wendy's Subway Book Prize as the Editors' Pick.**

The Passage Series is supported, in part, by public funds from the New York City Department of Cultural Affairs in partnership with the City Council.

Images in "Mandatory Fields" and "Bruise Smut": National Trust for Historic Preservation, "Prentice Women's Hospital Demolition Time Lapse," posted January 22, 2015, YouTube video, 01:55.